I0486264

The
Mortgage
Book

Most people think their Home,
is their most expensive purchase

Their Most Expensive Purchase is,
Their MORTGAGE!

BONUS!
10 Steps To
Repair Your Credit!

By

Oliver P. Maldonado

WWW.OliverMaldonado.com

ISBN: 978-1-4140-3665-6 (sc)
ISBN: 978-1-4140-3666-3 (e)

1stBooks - rev. 10/23/25

Table of Contents

Dedication

This book is dedicated to one of the most important people in my life, my daughter Isabelle Cecilia Maldonado who inspires me to be a better person and contribute to the community by changing the way business is done.

Acknowledgements

I would also like to acknowledge my mother Zaida Luz Ortiz who has been a great inspiration to me and who has also given me the values I live by today and practice in my business life. With out her influence and determination, I would not have been able to contribute to all of the lives I have helped and worked with over the years.

Authors Guarantee

My guarantee to current homeowners and mortgage buyers.
I guarantee that every home owner who reads this book will save thousands of dollars over the course of their mortgage and or future refinancing or I'll buy the book back from you!

You will be able to get immediate gratification in savings with the benefit of the bi-weekly payments which will accelerate your equity and shorten the term of your mortgage by 3-5 even 10 years. This would be the equivalent of $10,000-$20,000 even $50,000 plus of interest savings.

My guarantee to future homeowners!
I guarantee to any and all future homeowners the savings of thousands of dollars of closings costs on a home purchase. You'll also be able to save tens of thousands over the term of the mortgage by selecting the right mortgage first and the use of bi-weekly payments to accelerate your equity and shorten your mortgage term by 3-5 even 10 years.

By reading this book, you'll have all of the information needed to make a well informed educated decision regarding one of the most important financial decision you'll ever make.
You will not be taken advantage of, but this book will teach you how to get the best possible rates and closing costs and maybe even help you take advantage or exploit mortgage lenders and brokers. There are many lenders and brokers who've tried to stop me from writing this book. Many of whom have expressed their resentment towards the book since it reveals so much regarding this topic.

The Author will pay One Million Dollars ($1,000,000.00) of closing costs per state!

The author will pay, lower or refund up to one million ($1,000,000.00) dollars of closing costs per state (states are limited) for some states at $500 per funded mortgage done with him or one of his affiliates!

The Author will pay $500 of your closing costs

Oliver P. Maldonado will pay $500 of your next refinance or home mortgage done with him or one of his affiliated lenders or brokers.

Any and all mortgages done with the author carries his mortgage guarantee. He guarantees all of his clients the lowest interest rates and closing costs and will beat any legitimate Good Faith Estimate from another lender. Oliver P. Maldonado can do any and all mortgages under the sun and will not only guarantee you the lowest interest rates and closing costs but will also put you into the right mortgage program for your exact situation.

The author also guarantees that you will not have to pay an origination fee or any discount points on any and all future mortgages done after the first one with him.

You will not find another guarantee like this one anywhere in the mortgage industry!

The author will pay, lower or refund up to one million ($1,000,000.00) dollars of closing costs per state (states are limited) for some states at $500 per funded mortgage done with him or one of his affiliates!

$500 Gift Voucher

IMPORTANT FINANCIAL NOTICE TO
ALL WHO READ THIS BOOK!

The Author Oliver P. Maldonado has included this $500 Gift Voucher that can be used towards the closing costs of a mortgage done with him or one of his affiliates.

The bearer of this GIFT VOUCHER can use it to receive $500 DOLLARS off, towards or refunded from their next mortgage done with the author or one of his affiliates.

- You can lower your monthly payments up to 40% of your current high interest credit card debt
- You can receive cash to use for any reason
- Possible tax deduction (consult with your tax advisor)
- 24 To 48 hour Pre-Approvals
- No Equity? No Problem
- 2nds to 125% of value
- Bad Credit or Bankruptcy -ok-
- We have over 25 different programs available to fit almost anyone's situation CONFORMATION **# 3986**

Completely fill out this form and fax to 812-339-6554 the Publisher Attention: To the Author of "The Mortgage Book" Oliver P. Maldonado.

Borrower Name	Social Security #

C0-Borrower Name	Social Security #

Address			State	Zip Code
$_____	$_____	_____%		ARM Y / N
Current Balance	Mtg. Payment	Rate		(Circle One)

$_____

Employer	Income	How Long

$_____

Co-Borrower Employer	Co-Borrower Income	How Long

Limited to some states and limited amount. Some restrictions apply   NO CASH VALUE

Authors Guarantee

"My guarantee to current homeowners and mortgage buyers.
I guarantee that every home owner who reads this book will save thousands of dollars over the course of their mortgage and or future refinancing or I'll buy the book back at double what you paid for it!"

Introduction

For years homeowners have been miss lead & miss informed. Homeowners have been taught from way back when that the most important (Expensive) financial decision they will ever make would be buying their home right? **WRONG!**

That is the miss conception!

This way of thinking costs hundreds of thousands of homeowners around the country hundreds of millions of dollars in unnecessary interest payments and closing costs.

In actuality the average homeowner will pay almost double the cost of the home itself on the mortgage. They'll do this on the interest payments on the mortgage. So the mortgage is the most important financial decision the average homeowner will make. Not the home.

Let me give you an example, an average mortgage with a balance of $125,000 with an 8.50% interest rate at the average term of 30 years (360 months) will cost the homeowner $221,011.07 in interest alone!!

That means you will pay a total of $346,011.07 over the 30 year term!!

Now you tell me, what is the most important financial decision you will ever make. Your home or your mortgage?

Unfortunately, I have seen thousands of homeowners over the years that did not understand this concept & time & time again it has cost them. I have seen homeowners spend weeks even months shopping for the right home with the right color in the right neighborhood & not buy the home because they did not like the toilet.
I have seen these same homeowners suddenly find the right house & they feel as if they must close very quickly and wham they spent a whole hour checking up on just two mortgage companies & feel as if they have the right one.

WHAT? Are you kidding me!

They spent months looking for the right house & even did not buy one because of the toilet & then they spend only an hour looking for a mortgage company, is that what you're telling me?
Yes, I have seen it unfortunately way too often. This is the same type of homeowner that ends up with the wrong type of company with the wrong type of mortgage that call me crying. It is the same type of homeowner that just closed on the home of their dreams with the right toilet with a mortgage of $145,000 with an interest rate of 9.50% which will cost them $293,925.89 of interest alone.

Think about it.

"For years homeowners have been miss lead & miss informed. Homeowners have been taught from way back when that the most important (Expensive) financial decision they will ever make would be buying their home right? **WRONG!"**

"It's your mortgage! Your mortgage is the most expensive purchase you will ever make!"

If they would have just spent a lot more time looking for the right mortgage company instead they might of gotten the house with the wrong toilet, & once they found me. I would have given them the right mortgage of $145,000 at 8.50% & I would have saved them $37,552.16 over the life of the mortgage. This would easily pay for a whole new bathroom which would mean they would get rid of that nasty toilet they hated. In the end they would be loving me!

Get the picture?

Most homeowners have been miss lead over the years to believe the home is the most important financial decision they would ever make, when in fact their mortgage is the most important financial decision they will make.
I have actually seen people look harder for a real estate agent even though the main majority of them have the same fees or very similar fees, even if you pick the wrong real estate agent you may over pay a few hundred dollars give or take a little.
How ever if you pick the wrong lender & end up with the wrong type of program it will cost you many thousands of dollars in the closing costs alone, not to mention ten's of thousands of dollars over the life of the loan.

Chapter I.

Mortgages

To my surprise the majority of the thousands of people I've helped over the years have always been under the impression that their home is the most expensive and important purchase of their life. To this day this continues to be the fallacy of most homeowners I work with.

Don't take my word for it. See for yourself. Just ask several of your friends and family members which is their most expensive purchase or financial decision they'll ever make? Most likely 9 out of 10 of them will respond with the all too famous words "My home is the most expensive purchase". That would be WRONG!

The mortgage is the most important purchase!

Allow me to explain, better yet let me demonstrate it for you.

A $200,000 home with a 7.25% fixed interest rate at the average term of 30 years will actually cost the homeowner $488,217.60!

That can't be right! Can it? Indeed it can be and I hate to admit it, but it's absolutely true!

In this example you'll pay $288,217.60 in interest payments alone! You'll pay more on interest payments than the home itself, so as I've told thousands of people. Your mortgage is the most important financial decision most people will make while under the miss interpretation that its actually their home.

Let me give you a different example!

Jack & Shirley are thinking of buying a $200,000 home. They don't have $200,000 in the bank so they'll have to borrow the money in the form of a mortgage. They have good credit and earn a good living.

So far they have a pre-approval on there home with their current bank. They haven't shoped for a mortgage since they already know they have good credit and they've established a relationship with their banker over the past 8 years. Jack and Shirley think they couldn't possible get a better rate and closing costs than with their own bank.

This is Jack and Shirleys first mistake! They're not even sure what types of mortgages their bank offer, or even if its right for them. This could be a costly mistake which usually is, and what you don't know can hurt you!

Let's take a look at Jack and Shirleys pre-approval. They've been pre-approved for a mortgage amount of $200,000 at 6.75%. Jack and Shirley have a good relationship with their banker and their banker or loan officer was kind enough to give them the option of 6.75% fixed with no points, or 6.00% fixed with 1 point (1% of loan amount) to buy the rate down to 6.00%.

"A $200,000 home with a 7.25% fixed interest rate at the average term of 30 years will actually cost the homeowner $488,217.60!"

"In this example you'll pay $288,217.60 in interest payments alone! You'll pay more on interest payments than the home itself, so as I've told thousands of people. Your mortgage is the most important financial decision most people will make while under the miss interpretation that it's actually their home."

Jack and Shirley are very pleased to have been given the option.

Jack & Shirley think it over and realize that 1% of $200,000 is $2,000 that will be tacked on to the loan! Why would they want to pay an extra $2,000?

Lets analyze that for a moment. The monthly P&I payment at 6.75% is $1,289.94 that's with no points.
The monthly P&I payment at 6.00% with 1 point which is 1% of the loan amount which adds up to $2,000 would be $1,193.14. Hmm?

Can you see the problem here?
Well lets go a little deeper.
The difference in the monthly P&I payment is $96.80. Not too much to matter, right? WRONG!!! This is a huge mistake to go this route to just save $2,000? Don't get me wrong! $2,000 is a significant amount, but lets do the math.

$96.80 x 12 months = $1,161.60 Not a big deal right? WRONG!

When you think of interest rates, please think of them in long term not short term. Remember the average mortgage term is 30 years! That's 360 months! So if you want an accurate picture, you'd have to multiply the $1,161.60 times 30 which is the 30 years which adds up to a whopping $34,848!! No that's significantly more than a messley $2,000! Right? Right!

Let's do the math together.

$96.80 more per month x 12 months = $1,161.60 per year x 30 years = $34,848!! What?

Who would do this? Why would a couple like Jack & Shirley do this, you might be asking your self right now. The answer is simple, because someone sold it to them and they weren't aware of the consequences. They we're thinking they were saving $2,000 on their loan, and didn't realize how much it would cost them over time.

You might be saying to yourself right now that this would never happen to you, but believe me when I tell you. I see this every day! I try to talk my clients out of it and to buy the rate down. This is one of the best things I can teach my clients! After I explain it to them on paper and they see it for themselves is when they get this weird look on their face and realize the mistake they almost made. I then see a sigh of relief, and then typically a thank you!

There's a saying in the mortgage business that goes like this, "Pay me now or pay me later, but you're gonna pay me".

Sad but true. While this person you were dealing with didn't do anything wrong, the lender makes more money, obviously with a higher rate. The loan officer or person you were dealing with also made more money in commissions by giving you a higher rate. The lender will pay more for higher rates as a way of saying thank you to the loan officer, broker or mortgage professional.

What is a mortgage?

What is a mortgage? Good question. Simple put, a mortgage is a home loan! That's it! It's as simple as that. If the home was an auto, the mortgage would be an auto loan.

It seems that for many years the mortgage industry has always found ways to try and confuse and complicate something as simple as a mortgage. That's why they've come up with these complicated sounding terms such as a mortgage. Terms such as the Good Faith Estimate also known as the GFE, the Truth In Lending, also known as the TIL, Deed of Trust, Note, Escrows, Points, Caps, etc, etc, etc...

We'll cover these terms in more detail in the coming up chapters, but for now. Know that its no coincidence that the industry itself starts out by using a complicated term like "Mortgage" in order to scare consumers into believing that everything about it is difficult, when in actuality its very simple.

Oliver P. Maldonado

Once again, a mortgage is a mortgage is a mortgage! Get it?

It's very simple when you think of it!

Let me go into more detail.
A mortgage requires you to put your home up as security (collateral) for repayment of your loan the mortgage. The lender will hold the title which is a lien on your property until you have paid back the principal plus interest. If you do not repay the mortgage, the lender has the right to take possession of the house by foreclosing and sell it in order to satisfy the mortgage.

Now there is one thing that is familiar with every mortgage under the sun. Every mortgage in the country starts at the same place, the mortgage application.

This application is also known as the 1003, also referenced as the (Ten O Three), or the Uniform residential Mortgage Application (URLA). This application is universal as in the name. This means that it's the same application whether you were applying for a mortgage in Colorado, Florida or New York. As far as the mortgage application goes, it will be and look the same for each state. Now, that does not necessarily apply for the state regulations and laws. Each state has it's own rules and regulations that might differ. That being said, remember that a mortgage is a mortgage is a mortgage. Meaning all FHA mortgages have to comply with the Fannie Mae and Freddie Macks rules and guidelines. The same goes for Conventional and all conforming mortgage loans.

Fannie Mae and Freddie Mack are the organizations that regulate the mortgage industry and have set the rules and guidelines for it.

Following will be an example of the 1003, Uniform Residential Loan Application (URLA) which consists of 4 pages.

Uniform Residential Loan Application

This application is designed to be completed by the applicant(s) with the lender's assistance. Applicants should complete this form as "Borrower" or "Co-Borrower", as applicable. Co-Borrower information must also be provided (and the appropriate box checked) when ☐ the income or assets of a person other than the "Borrower" (including the Borrower's spouse) will be used as a basis for loan qualification or ☐ the income or assets of the Borrower's spouse will not be used as a basis for loan qualification, but his or her liabilities must be considered because the Borrower resides in a community property state, the security property is located in a community property state, or the Borrower is relying on other property located in a community property state as a basis for repayment of the loan.

I. TYPE OF MORTGAGE AND TERMS OF LOAN

Mortgage Applied for:	☐ V.A. ☑ Conventional ☐ Other: ☐ FHA ☐ FmHA		Agency Case Number		Lender Case Number
Amount $ 223,000	Interest Rate 7.250 %	No. of Months 360/360	Amortization Type: ☑ Fixed Rate ☐ GPM	Other (explain): ☐ ARM (type):	

II. PROPERTY INFORMATION AND PURPOSE OF LOAN

Subject Property Address (street, city, state, ZIP) 123 Colorado Drive, Denver, CO 80221	No. of Units
Legal Description of Subject Property (attach description if necessary)	Year Built

Purpose of Loan ☑ Purchase ☐ Refinance ☐ Construction ☐ Construction-Permanent ☐ Other (explain):	Property will be: ☑ Primary Residence ☐ Secondary Residence ☐ Investment

Complete this line if construction or construction-permanent loan.

Year Lot Acquired	Original Cost $	Amount Existing Liens $	(a) Present Value of Lot $	(b) Cost of Improvements $	Total (a+b) $

Complete this line if this is a refinance loan.

Year Acquired	Original Cost $	Amount Existing Liens $	Purpose of Refinance	Describe Improvements ☐ made ☐ to be made Cost $

Title will be held in what Name(s)	Manner in which Title will be held	Estate will be held in: ☑ Fee Simple
Source of Down Payment, Settlement Charges and/or Subordinate Financing (explain)		☐ Leasehold (show expiration date)

III. BORROWER INFORMATION

Borrower	Co-Borrower
Borrower's Name (include Jr. or Sr. if applicable) Jack Borrower	Co-Borrower's Name (include Jr. or Sr. if applicable) Shirley Borrower
Social Security Number 123-45-6789 Home Phone (incl. area code) 000-000-0000 Age Yrs. School	Social Security Number Home Phone (incl. area code) Age Yrs. School
☐ Married ☐ Unmarried (include single, divorced, widowed) ☐ Separated Dependents (not listed by Co-Borrower) no. ages	☐ Married ☐ Unmarried (include single, divorced, widowed) ☐ Separated Dependents (not listed by Borrower) no. ages
Present Address (street, city, state, ZIP) ☐ Own ☐ Rent ___ No. Yrs. 123 Colorado Drive Denver, CO 80221	Present Address (street, city, state, ZIP) ☐ Own ☐ Rent ___ No. Yrs.

If residing at present address for less than two years, complete the following:

Former Address (street, city, state, ZIP) ☐ Own ☐ Rent ___ No. Yrs.	Former Address (street, city, state, ZIP) ☐ Own ☐ Rent ___ No. Yrs.
Former Address (street, city, state, ZIP) ☐ Own ☐ Rent ___ No. Yrs.	Former Address (street, city, state, ZIP) ☐ Own ☐ Rent ___ No. Yrs.

IV. EMPLOYMENT INFORMATION

Borrower	Co-Borrower
Name and Address of Employer ☐ Self Employed Yrs. on this job	Name and Address of Employer ☐ Self Employed Yrs. on this job
Yrs. employed in this line of work/profession	Yrs. employed in this line of work/profession
Position/Title/Type of Business Business Phone (incl. area code)	Position/Title/Type of Business Business Phone (incl. area code)

If employed in current position for less than two years or if currently employed in more than one position, complete the following:

Name and Address of Employer ☐ Self Employed Dates(from-to)	Name and Address of Employer ☐ Self Employed Dates(from-to)
Monthly Income $	Monthly Income $
Position/Title/Type of Business Business Phone (incl. area code)	Position/Title/Type of Business Business Phone (incl. area code)
Name and Address of Employer ☐ Self Employed Dates(from-to)	Name and Address of Employer ☐ Self Employed Dates(from-to)
Monthly Income $	Monthly Income $
Position/Title/Type of Business Business Phone (incl. area code)	Position/Title/Type of Business Business Phone (incl. area code)

Freddie Mac Form 65 10/92	Page 1 of 4 Borrower _____	Fannie Mae Form 1003 10/92
CALYX Form 1003 Loanapp1 hp 2/95	Co-Borrower _____	

Oliver P. Maldonado

V. MONTHLY INCOME AND COMBINED HOUSING EXPENSE INFORMATION

Gross Monthly Income	Borrower	Co-Borrower	Total	Combined Monthly Housing Expense	Present	Proposed
Base Empl. Income*	$	$	$	Rent	$	$
Overtime				First Mortgage (P&I)		1,521.25
Bonuses				Other Financing (P&I)		
Commissions				Hazard Insurance		
Dividends/Interest				Real Estate Taxes		
Net Rental Income				Mortgage Insurance		
Other (before completing, see the notice in "Describe other income," below)				Homeowner Assn. Dues		
				Other		
Total	$	$	$	Total	$	$ 1,521.25

*Self Employed Borrower(s) may be required to provide additional documentation such as tax returns and financial statements.

Describe Other Income Notice: Alimony, child support, or separate maintenance income need not be revealed if the Borrower(B) or Co-Borrower(C) does not choose to have it considered for repaying this loan.

B/C		Monthly Amount
		$

VI. ASSETS AND LIABILITIES

This statement and any applicable supporting schedules may be completed jointly by both married and unmarried Co-borrowers if their assets and liabilities are sufficiently joined so that the Statement can be meaningfully and fairly presented on a combined basis; otherwise separate Statements and Schedules are required. If the Co-Borrower section was completed about a spouse, this Statement and supporting schedules must be completed about that spouse also.

Completed ☑ Jointly ☐ Not Jointly

ASSETS Description	Cash or Market Value	Liabilities and Pledged Assets. List the creditor's name, address and account number for all outstanding debts, including automobile loans, revolving charge accounts, real estate loans, alimony, child support, stock pledges, etc. Use continuation sheet, if necessary. Indicate by (*) those liabilities which will be satisfied upon sale of real estate owned or upon refinancing of the subject property.	Monthly Payt. & Mos. Left to Pay	Unpaid Balance
Cash deposit toward purchase held by	$	**LIABILITIES**		
		Name and address of Company	$ Payt./Mos.	$
List checking and savings accounts below				
Name and address of Bank, S&L, or Credit Union				
		Acct. no.		
		Name and address of Company	$ Payt./Mos.	$
Acct. no.	$			
Name and address of Bank, S&L, or Credit Union				
		Acct. no.		
		Name and address of Company	$ Payt./Mos.	$
Acct. no.	$			
Name and address of Bank, S&L, or Credit Union				
		Acct. no.		
		Name and address of Company	$ Payt./Mos.	$
Acct. no.	$			
Name and address of Bank, S&L, or Credit Union				
		Acct. no.		
		Name and address of Company	$ Payt./Mos.	$
Acct. no.	$			
Stocks & Bonds (Company name/ number & description)	$			
		Acct. no.		
		Name and address of Company	$ Payt./Mos.	$
Life insurance net cash value				
Face amount: $	$			
Subtotal Liquid Assets	$			
Real estate owned (enter market value from schedule of real estate owned)	$	Acct. no.		
Vested interest in retirement fund	$	Name and address of Company	$ Payt./Mos.	$
Net worth of business(es) owned (attach financial statement)	$			
Automobiles owned (make and year)	$			
		Acct. no.		
		Alimony/Child Support/Separate Maintenance Payments Owed to:	$	
Other Assets (itemize)	$	Job Related Expense (child care, union dues, etc.)	$	
		Total Monthly Payments	$	
Total Assets a.	$	**Net Worth (a-b)**	$	**Total Liabilities b.** $

Freddie Mac Form 65   10/92
CALYX Form 1003 Loanapp2 hp 2/95

Page 2 of 4   Borrower _____   Fannie Mae Form 1003   10/92
Co-Borrower _____

8

VI. ASSETS AND LIABILITIES (cont.)

Schedule of Real Estate Owned (if additional properties are owned, use continuation sheet)

Property Address (enter S if sold, PS if pending sale or R if rental being held for income)	Type of Property	Present Market Value	Amount of Mortgages & Liens	Gross Rental Income	Mortgage Payments	Insurance, Maintenance Taxes & Misc	Net Rental Income
		$	$	$	$	$	$
Totals		$	$	$	$	$	$

List any additional names under which credit has previously been received and indicate appropriate creditor name(s) and account number(s):

Alternate Name | Creditor Name | Account Number

VII. DETAILS OF TRANSACTION

a. Purchase price	$
b. Alterations, improvements, repairs	
c. Land (if acquired separately)	
d. Refinance (incl. debts to be paid off)	
e. Estimated prepaid items	134.73
f. Estimated closing costs	4,769.50
g. PMI, MIP, Funding Fee	
h. Discount (if Borrower will pay)	1,115.00
i. Total costs (add items a through h)	6,019.23
j. Subordinate financing	
k. Borrower's closing costs paid by Seller	
l. Other Credits (explain)	
m. Loan amount (exclude PMI, MIP, Funding Fee financed)	223,000.00
n. PMI, MIP, Funding Fee financed	
o. Loan amount (add m & n)	223,000.00
p. Cash from/to Borrower (subtract j, k, l & o from i)	(216,980.77)

VIII. DECLARATIONS

If you answer "yes" to any questions a through i, please use continuation sheet for explanation.

Borrower Yes No / Co-Borrower Yes No

a. Are there any outstanding judgments against you?
b. Have you been declared bankrupt within the past 7 years?
c. Have you had property foreclosed upon or given title or deed in lieu thereof in the last 7 years?
d. Are you a party to a lawsuit?
e. Have you directly or indirectly been obligated on any loan which resulted in foreclosure, transfer of title in lieu of foreclosure, or judgment? (This would include such loans as home mortgage loans, SBA loans, home improvement loans, educational loans, manufactured (mobile) home loans, any mortgage, financial obligation, bond, or loan guarantee. If "Yes," provide details, including date, name and address of Lender, FHA or VA case number, if any, and reasons for the action.)
f. Are you presently delinquent or in default on any Federal debt or any other loan, mortgage, financial obligation bond, or loan guarantee? If "Yes," give details as described in the preceding question.
g. Are you obligated to pay alimony, child support, or separate maintenance?
h. Is any part of the down payment borrowed?
i. Are you a co-maker or endorser on a note?
j. Are you a U. S. citizen?
k. Are you a permanent resident alien?
l. Do you intend to occupy the property as your primary residence? If "Yes," complete question m below.
m. Have you had an ownership interest in a property in the last three years?
(1) What type of property did you own-principal residence (PR), second home (SH), or investment property (IP)?
(2) How did you hold title to the home-solely by yourself (S), jointly with your spouse (SP), or jointly with another person (O)?

IX. ACKNOWLEDGMENT AND AGREEMENT

The undersigned specifically acknowledge(s) and agree(s) that: (1) the loan requested by this application will be secured by a first mortgage or deed of trust on the property described herein; (2) the property will not be used for any illegal or prohibited purpose or use; (3) all statements made in this application are made for the purpose of obtaining the loan indicated herein; (4) occupation of the property will be as indicated above; (5) verification or reverification of any information contained in the application may be made at any time by the Lender, its agents, successors and assigns, either directly or through a credit reporting agency, from any source named in this application, and the original copy of this application will be retained by the Lender, even if the loan is not approved; (6) the Lender, its agents, successors and assigns will rely on the information contained in the application and I/we have a continuing obligation to amend and/or supplement the information provided in this application if any of the material facts which I/we have represented herein should change prior to closing; (7) in the event my/our payments on the loan indicated in this application become delinquent, the Lender, its agents, successors and assigns, may, in addition to all their other rights and remedies, report my/our name(s) and account information to a credit reporting agency; (8) ownership of the loan may be transferred to successor or assign of the Lender without notice to me and/or the administration of the loan account may be transferred to an agent, successor or assign of the Lender with prior notice to me; (9) the Lender, its agents, successors and assigns make no representations or warranties, express or implied, to the Borrower(s) regarding the condition of the property, or the value of the property.
Certification: I/We certify that the information provided in this application is true and correct as of the date set forth opposite my/our signature(s) on this application and acknowledge my/our understanding that any intentional or negligent misrepresentation(s) of the information contained in this application may result in civil liability and/or criminal penalties including, but not limited to, fine or imprisonment or both under the provisions of Title 18, United States Code, Section 1001, et seq. and liability for monetary damages to the Lender, its agents, successors and assigns, insurers and any other person who may suffer any loss due to reliance upon any misrepresentation which I/we have made on this application.

Borrower's Signature | Date | Co-Borrower's Signature | Date

X | X

X. INFORMATION FOR GOVERNMENT MONITORING PURPOSES

The following information is requested by the Federal Government for certain types of loans related to a dwelling, in order to monitor the Lender's compliance with equal credit opportunity, fair housing and home mortgage disclosure laws. You are not required to furnish this information, but are encouraged to do so. The law provides that a Lender may neither discriminate on the basis of this information, nor on whether you choose to furnish it. However, if you choose not to furnish it, under Federal regulations this Lender is required to note race and sex on the basis of visual observation or surname. If you do not wish to furnish the above information, please check the box below. (Lender must review the above material to assure that the disclosure satisfy all requirements to which the Lender is subject under applicable state law for the particular type of loan applied for.)

BORROWER — I do not wish to furnish this information
Race/National Origin: American Indian or Alaskan Native / Asian or Pacific Islander / Black, not of Hispanic origin / White, not of Hispanic origin / Hispanic / Other (specify)
Sex: Female / Male

CO-BORROWER — I do not wish to furnish this information
Race/National Origin: American Indian or Alaskan Native / Asian or Pacific Islander / Black, not of Hispanic origin / White, not of Hispanic origin / Hispanic / Other (specify)
Sex: Female / Male

To be Completed by Interviewer | Interviewer's Name (print or type): **Oliver P. Maldonado**
This application was taken by: face-to-face interview / by mail / by telephone
Interviewer's Signature | Date
Interviewer's Phone Number (incl. area code)
Name and Address Interviewer's Employer

Please take a good look and study the 1003 mortgage application. As I mentioned before all mortgages start here.

Incorrect information on the mortgage application.

The information contained in this application will be the deciding factor whether a mortgage is approved or denied. Most problems, I would estimate about 90% of all mortgage mistakes are done here on the application. Most problems that slow down the process or the mortgage loan is because the information on this application is either entered wrong, supplied wrong.
On many occasions it is not even through the fault of your own. Some information is entered by the mortgage professional and not you the client. This is information as far as the loan type, rate type, term, etc. If this information is entered improperly, then it could mean the difference of qualifying or nor for a mortgage loan.

This is why it is imperative to do business with the right mortgage professional. Notice how I mentioned right mortgage professional and not mortgage company. Even the good mortgage companies hire newbie's that are still inexperienced and don't know the mortgage industry.

Now keep in mind that the mortgage professional is hopefully not going to enter the information on the applications incorrect on purpose. They may have even entered the information as correct as they know, it would only be because they do not know or understand the business well enough. They entered for a program that is not doable? Or they may have entered the information for a program that they don't understand, or even a program that the client might not qualify for.

This could be something as simple as for instance; If they entered the interest rate for an FHA as a 3/1 ARM, they would not qualify because this program doesn't exist. See FHA's do not have a 3/1 ARM. The 3/1 ARM is a conventional product, so it would get denied. Especially if this was entered electronically. Now this is a doable mortgage, but since the information is entered incorrect it would get denied.

Now if no one tells this mortgage person that they entered the information wrong and if he does not catch it, he would call the client back and say they were not able to qualify as they thought. When the client asks why, most likely the person will make something up because they also do not understand why.

Another example is if they stated the mortgage to be a no cash out refinance and there is cash out because they are combining a 1st and 2nd mortgage then this would be a cash out refinance. This is a doable mortgage, but once again because the information is entered incorrect it would not get approved this way and may take some time to figure out why.

So remember, it is very important to be dealing with the right mortgage professional. It could make the difference between qualifying and getting denied for a mortgage loan.

What makes a mortgage?

All mortgages are comprised of three things. Every mortgage no matter which one or what kind you're talking about has three things.

Every mortgage has a principal value also known as the balance. The principal loan amount will determine the Loan to Value (LTV). (We'll cover this term in the next chapters) Remember what a mortgage is. A mortgage is a home loan, so since it's a home loan it must have an amount. So the first thing every mortgage in the world must have is first of all a principal amount.

The second thing a mortgage must have is an interest rate. The interest rate will help determine the Debt to Income (DTI). Along with any and all other debt you may have that they know about. The interest rate is will also determine your monthly payment which is typically why everyone always talks about the rates. This alone isn't what the average homeowner or future homeowner should worry about. The interest rate is only a piece of the puzzle.

The interest rate is the second thing that will help in placing you into the right or type of mortgage. I know that most lenders and brokers would love to give you a mortgage, and some of the motivation for all lenders and brokers to want to give you a mortgage (Home Loan) is because of the interest rate. This is how they make their money and the reason they're willing to pay others (Brokers) to also lend you money.

This is where the P&I from PITI come from. The P&I stand for Principal and Interest. PITI in its entirety stands for Principal Interest Taxes and Insurance.

The third thing that makes a mortgage and determine the mortgage type is credit. That's right. There are so many programs and all of them require credit. It doesn't necessarily mean good or bad credit or even no credit. There are programs available for each one of these categories, but the question will always be. What kind of credit?
The credit will be the most important part of the mortgage, which will then determine the principal amount and interest.

Monthly Mortgage payments

PITI stands for Principal Interest Taxes and Insurance.

On an average 30 year (360 months) $150,000 mortgage at 7.00% interest the payment would be $992.17. I would love to tell everyone that this would be the total payment. But unfortunately this payment would only represent the P&I (Principal & Interest).

As you already know, you must pay taxes on everything you buy. This also applies to homes you purchase, so the next thing is taxes.

You must pay taxes on your home, and as you probable know, the taxes on a $150,000 home is going to be significant, so its customary for the taxes to be rolled into the mortgage and paid on a monthly basis. The taxes will depend in the county you live in and should be considered when thinking of buying a home. This can and will affect your monthly payments.

The last I in PITI would stand for Insurance. Yes, you must have insurance on the home just like when you buy a car. What lender is going to lend you $150,000 and not have homeowners insurance in case something happened to the collateral? Not many!

Don't confuse this type of insurance MI which is Mortgage insurance or to PMI Private Mortgage Insurance.
MI and PMI is insurance, but this type of insurance isn't your typical homeowners insurance. Regular homeowners insurance protects the home. MI and PMI protects the lender in case something happens to you? Well not necessarily to you, but in case you stop paying on your mortgage the lender will be covered.
MI is typically for mortgages above the 80% LTV range and PMI is for FHA mortgages regardless of LTV.

Okay so lets review.
The first thing a mortgage has is a Principal amount.
The second thing a mortgage must have is an interest rate.
Last but not least is the third item that all mortgages need in order to determine the type and kind of mortgage is CREDIT!

Of the three things, credit would most likely be the most important one of all.

The last thing that will determine the mortgage payment is the term. The average mortgage term is 30 years which is 360 months. If you only had a principal loan and interest rate, you wouldn't be able to calculate what your payments would be unless you knew what the term is. There are also 20, 15 and 10 year mortgage terms.

The mortgage payment is also known as the amortization. The amounts of payments you will make on your principal and interest are calculated to let you buy your home for a fixed period of time. During the first few years to even half of the term, most of your payments will be applied toward the interest you owe. During the later term of your loan, your payments will then go towards the principal. This type of repayment is known as amortization.

Types of mortgages

There are many, many types of mortgages. As you read this it is very important for you to remember and understand that all mortgages no matter what type or kind are comprised of three things.
Those again are the Loan to Value (LTV), Debt to Income (DTI) and Credit.

Every mortgage in the world needs these three things in order to place into the right mortgage or to even know what type of mortgage to place into (Qualify).
Without knowing each of these three things, there is no way to know what kind of mortgage you would and can qualify for. This is a fact and be very careful of anyone that tells you otherwise.

For example, all too often I hear my soon too be clients tell me how someone has quoted them this rate what ever it might be. Or quoted them those closing costs.
My first question then is, have they pre-approved you? Have they given you a Good Faith Estimate in writing? If no, I'm almost positive that they we're quoted something by someone who most likely has not even seen their credit report yet. This quote is usually the switch and bait approach. There being quoted something that in most cases aren't very realistic? Or something was left out?

Lastly I'll ask if anyone has taken an application on them. I'll usually hear a no. Then I'll hear them ask what my rates are, and closing costs, etc.
I'll then start asking which program those quotes were for? Was that quote for a government loan? FHA or VA? Conventional? Once they've tried to answer that, I'll ask if they know what their LTV is? Or what their DTI is? After that, if there still quoting me what

someone else has misled them about, I'll end my probing questions with what are your credit scores.

By this time they've realized that maybe those other quotes aren't as good as they might have thought they were. This is also the time when they begin to understand that with out knowing what they're talking about that maybe they'll need to research the topic in more detail.

A prospect will usually begin asking me why I'm asking all of these questions and that no one else has asked them all of those questions.

I'll then begin explaining how it is impossible to quote rates, closing costs and programs without knowing each of these things.

What rate should I quote? A rate for someone with a 700 credit score? Or a rate for someone with a 450 credit score? A rate and closing costs on an FHA Purchase? Or Conventional refinance? A rate for someone self employed? Or???

This is also the point when my prospects start to become my clients. By this point they're starting to realize that if someone else has quoted them those rates and fees, that person may very well have been misleading them. If they weren't being misled, then they we're probable quoted something that realistically they may not even qualify for, which in my opinion is one of the same.

They begin to realize that they would rather work with someone who can explain the process and reasons for things so they can understand, which will give them the knowledge to be able to make an informed decision and not be taken advantage of.

They also realize that this decision starts by selecting the right person or company, me! This will in it self help them sleep better at night knowing I'm on their side.

Are you starting to see my point?

There is no such thing as a bad mortgage! Or good mortgage for that matter as well. There are the right programs and wrong programs for everyone, which in turn earn the names of bad or good mortgages.

Regardless of what mortgage a person might go into or need, each persons situation will be every different. Most have different goals in life. Be at different points in time. What I'm trying to say is that everyone will usually have different goals and needs and this will and should also affect their decision in the type of mortgage they're put into and or want.

I wish I could say that most loan officers, originators or brokers have the same knowledge, but the reality is, they don't. I wish I could also say that each of them are looking out for your best interest, but once again the reality is in many cases they're just looking out for themselves.

I hate to say it, but all too often I hear the horror stories and have even seen unscrupulous professionals put borrowers into the wrong program for them just because it was a program that would be quicker for them to earn their commissions. I've seen this even when they had the proper program available for the client, but just wanted to get paid sooner, regardless of it being the wrong program for their client.

It truly saddens me when I hear and or see it. I do the best I can to stop these things from happening in the industry and I hope this book helps not only consumers, but also the professionals that I haven't had the pleasure of training yet.

Okay that being said, lets start talking about the types of mortgages themselves. I hope you understand that it is necessary to understand what I've tried to communicate first, before we just start going over the types of mortgages.

FHA (Federal Housing Administration)

Although most think this is a government loan, in actuality it's a government insured (guaranteed) loan. The reason one would use an FHA mortgage is because it allows borrowers to go to a higher Loan to Value (LTV), higher Debt to Income Ratios (DTI) and borrowers don't have to have the best credit. This means that borrowers can qualify for more home for less money down.

An FHA mortgage is also an A paper mortgage so you'll typically have a lower rate and closing costs. Being federally insured and regulated any one getting an FHA mortgage will have the added protection of having to comply and obey stricter lending practices.

There are certain fees that lenders are not allowed to charge on FHA insured mortgages. Since an FHA mortgage is federally insured, there will be more attention paid to them so lenders and brokers are very careful as to what they do with FHA mortgages. This is an added advantage for people electing to get an FHA versus another mortgage.

Many lenders will limit what they make on an FHA mortgage along with how much brokers are allowed to make as well. Don't let this fool you though. Even though you'll have a lot more protection with an FHA mortgage, you can still be taken advantage of and may be overcharged, you'll just be guaranteed not to be taken to the cleaners, but you still may over pay, which can still cost you thousands.

Even though you're probable not going to overpay in closing costs, if you're given the wrong rate or a higher rate so the lender and or broker can earn more money, it can cost you tens of thousands in the long run.

Let me give you an example.

Let's say theres a couple named Jack & Shirley and they're going to get a 30 year FHA mortgage with a principal amount of $200,000. The lender has mentioned that they have the choice of getting a fixed

6.75% interest rate with no points, or they can pay 1 point (1%) and buy the rate down to 6.00%.

Jack and Shirley think about it and realize that 1% of $200,000 is $2,000 that will be tacked on to the loan! Why would they want to pay an extra $2,000?

Lets analyze that for a moment. The monthly P&I payment at 6.75% is $1,289.94 that's with no points. The monthly P&I payment at 6.00% with 1 point which is 1% of the loan amount which adds up to $2,000 would be $1,193.14.

Hmm?

Can you see the problem here?

Well lets go a little deeper. The difference in the monthly P&I payment is $96.80. Not too much to matter, right? WRONG!!! This is a huge mistake to go this route to just save $2,000? Don't get me wrong! $2,000 is a significant amount, but lets do the math.

$96.80 x 12 months = $1,161.60 Not a big deal right? WRONG!

When you think of interest rates, please think of them in long term not short term. Remember the average mortgage term is 30 years! That's 360 months! So if you want an accurate picture, you'd have to multiply the $1,161.60 times 30 which is the 30 years which adds up to a whopping $34,848!! No that's significantly more than a messley $2,000! Right? Right!

Let's do the math together.

$96.80 more per month x 12 months = $1,161.60 per year x 30 years = $34,848!! What?

Who would do this? Why would a couple like Jack & Shirley do this, you might be asking your self right now. The answer is simple, because someone sold it to them and they weren't aware of the consequences. They we're thinking they were saving $2,000 on their loan, and didn't realize how much it would cost them over time.

You might be saying to yourself right now that this would never happen to you, but believe me when I tell you. I see this every day! I try to talk my clients out of it and to buy the rate down. This is one of the best things I can teach my clients! After I explain it to them on paper and they see it for themselves is when they get this weird look on their face and realize the mistake they almost made. I then see a sigh of relief, and then typically a thank you!

There's a saying in the mortgage business that goes like this, "Pay me now or pay me later, but you're gonna pay me".

Sad but true. While this person you were dealing with didn't do anything wrong, the lender makes more money, obviously with a higher rate. The loan officer or person you were dealing with also made more money in commissions by giving you a higher rate. The lender will pay more for higher rates as a way of saying thank you!

With an FHA there is an Mortgage Insurance Premium (MIP Fee) of 1.50% of the loan amount tacked on to the loan. The MIP fee is 1.50% of the loan amount divided into five years. The MIP used to be 2.25% of the loan amount, but that changed in January of 2000 to 1.50%.

If you convert an FHA to a conventional the unused portion of the MIP fee is refundable.

There are a lot of homeowners under the misconception that if their LTV goes under 80% that the MIP fee would or could drop. That isn't the case for an FHA, but is the case for a conventional which we'll be covering a little bit later.
So just so there's no misunderstanding, there is an MIP fee with all FHA's for as long as you have it. The MIP fee is what makes it an FHA.

FHA will typically go up to 97% LTV with a 43% DTI and credit scores under 600.

Once again I'd like to give you an example using easy to follow numbers.

If you wanted to buy a home and wanted to try and qualify with an FHA mortgage, if you wanted to buy a $100,000 home, if you qualify you could get a mortgage of $97,000 which represents 97% LTV. Of coarse this would be less closing costs and pre-paids.

Mortgage	Devided Into	Home Value	Equals	
$97,000	/	$100,000	=	97% LTV

There are FHA loan limits which mean that the FHA loan can only go to a certain amount. This will vary by State & County.

FHA average loan limits by State for single family residences. Keep in mind that these are the averages and some counties in the states may vary.

Alabama	$154,896
Alaska	$190,000
Arizona	$154,896-$168,550
Arkansas	$154,896
California	$154,896-$280,749
Colorado	$154,896-261,609
Connecticut	$171,000-280,250
Delaware	$154,896-$192,288
District of Columbia	$154,896-$269,800
Florida	$154,896-$280,749
Georgia	$154,896-$176,605
Hawaii	$181,944-$327,750
Idaho	$154,896
Illinois	$154,896-$234,150
Indiana	$154,896-$180,405
Iowa	$154,986
Kansas	$154,896
Kentucky	$154,896-$180,405
Louisiana	$154,896
Maine	$154,896-$189,525

Maryland	$154,896-$269,800
Massachusetts	$170,362-$280,749
Michigan	$154,896-$209,000
Minnesota	$154,896-$218,405
Mississippi	$154,896
Missouri	$154,896-$185,420
Montana	$154,896
Nebraska	$154,896
Nevada	$154,896-$175,750
New Hampshire	$154,896-$280,749
New Jersey	$184,666-$280,749
New Mexico	$154,896-$242,250
New York	$154,896-$280,749
North Carolina	$154,896-$174,800
North Dakota	$154,896
Ohio	$154-896-$221,000
Oklahoma	$154,896
Oregon	$154,896-$185,155
Pennsylvania	$154,896-$184,666
Puerto Rico	$154,896-$247,000
Rhode Island	$199,500-$213,750
South Carolina	$154,896-$199,500
South Dakota	$154,896
Tennessee	$154,896-$226,100
Texas	$154,896-$177,650
Utah	$154,896-$171,000
Vermont	$154,896-$155,325
Virgin Islands	$187,300-$242,250
Virginia	$154,896-$269,800
Washington	$154,896-$248,420
West Virginia	$154,896-$269,800
Wisconsin	$154,896-$218,405
Wyoming	$154,896-$216,600

Conforming Mortgage Limit

All States	$333,700.00

Conforming and non conforming mortgages

What is a conforming mortgage? A conforming mortgage is a mortgage that conforms to government standards and guidelines. One of them being the loan limit. A conforming loan limit means that in order to qualify as a conforming loan, it must not go over a certain mortgage loan amount. The reason one would want a conforming loan is because they would benefit from the best rates around.

Non-Conforming Mortgages / Jumbo Loans

Anything above and over the conforming mortgage loan limit would be considered a Jumbo loan which is a non-conforming mortgage. Non conforming mortgages typically have higher interest rates.

Conventional Mortgages

A conventional mortgage is a conforming mortgage which means it conforms to FANNIE MAE and FREDDIE MACK guidelines. These are two organizations that regulate the mortgage industry.

Conventional mortgages will go to 95% LTV and have a DTI of 42%. If you have a higher LTV or DTI, you'd want to think of an FHA. You also need a little better credit when doing a conventional. The minimum credit scores are usually 620.

Conventional and FHA mortgages are conforming loans which mean they confirm to government guidelines. Each of these have loan limits and anything above the limits would put it into a different category known as JUMBO loans. This type of loan is a non confirming loan, because it doesn't confirm to the loan limits set by the governing organizations.

This is typically the types of conventional mortgages. Be careful when communicating with other professionals. There are many, many consumers and professionals alike that will speak of mortgages and if it's not an FHA or VA mortgage, they're consider it a conventional mortgage. Is it wrong? Yes, no, maybe? It really doesn't matter what kind of mortgage they call it. It only matters that you understand the difference. It's important for you top identify what type of mortgage you are getting so you know what you should be charged as far as fees go and also what type of rate to expect.

What type of Adjustable, or fixed rate. If you do not know what type of mortgage you are getting, then how could you possible know about the closing costs or rate?

What is equity?

Equity is the difference between the loan balance and the value of the home. In other words it's the loan amount or balance minus the value of the home. The difference is the equity.

Let me try to break it down for you. I'll use easy numbers to follow with.

Lets say you have a mortgage balance (Loan Amount) of $80,000 and lets say that the home value is $100,000. If you subtract the loan amount and the value this is what the equity is.

Loan Amount	Minus	Value	Equals	Equity
$80,000	-	$100,000	=	$20,000

In the example you will see that the difference of the mortgage balance and the value is the sweet equity.

A homeowner can use their equity as collateral for 2nd mortgages, secured loans, cash out, etc. Typically the equity of homes is used for 2nd mortgages.

2nd Mortgages

So typically a 2nd mortgage will use the equity as security. So in the example above if you wanted to use a part of the $20,000 you have in equity, or even in some cases you could use 100% of your equity for a 2nd mortgage you could. Of course like all mortages you'll have to qualify for it and not every one can qualify up to 100% Combined Loan To Value (CLTV). Also like all mortgages not every one has that type of 2nd mortgages available.

125% Loan To Value 2nd Mortgages

The 125% LTV mortgage has become almost extinct. This is the type of mortgage that brought me into the business. It's a great mortgage but I wouldn't recommend it to everyone. Only certain people in certain situations should consider this type of mortgage. Although the veterans in the business really never liked the 125% LTV 2nd mortgage, I have to stick up for them. I've helped literally hundreds if not thousands of people with these 125% LTV 2nd mortgages. I've helped people keep their homes and not have to file bankruptcy with this type of mortgage. I've helped people that have had major family emergencies and had to max out all of their credit cards during these crisis's. That's on the personal side.

On the business side, these mortgages out performed all analysts expectations. Each of these mortgages were typically paid in full before the term of the mortgage, well ahead of the scheduled pay off. Most people who did a 125% LTV 2nd mortgage rarely if ever got back into tough situations. Most 125% LTV 2nd mortgages were paid for and did not become delinquent mortgages.

So I must stick up for these and if you're over extended, then you should consider a 125% LTV 2nd mortgage if you can qualify for it.

So what is a 125% LTV 2nd mortgage? Well you're starting to learn enough about the industry and mortgages to figure it out, but let me indulge you.

A 125% LTV 2nd Mortgage is a mortgage that will go up to 125% Loan TO Value. Yep, you read that right. So these mortgages will give you more than the home is worth.

For instance,

Loan Amount	Devided	Value	Equals	LTV
$100,000	/	$100,000	=	100% LTV

In this example there is no equity. So with the typical 2nd mortgage equity loan there is no space to do anything.

But with a 125% CLTV 2nd mortgage, this is what it could look like.

Loan Amount	Times	Value	Equals	Equity
$100,000	*125%	$100,000	=	$125,000 CLTV

So in other words;

	Loan Amount	Devided	Value	Equals	LTV
1st Mtg	$100,000	/	$100,000	=	100%

But you'd be able to qualify for a 2nd 125% LTV mortgage of $25,000. So here's how a 125% LTV would look like;

	Loan Amount	Devided	Value	Equals	LTV
1st Mtg	$100,000	/	$100,000	=	100%
2nd Mtg	$25,000	/	$25,000	=	125%
CLTV					

Get it? It should be pretty simple to understand. If you don't then contact a mortgage professional to explain it in more detail.

Every mortgage has three things that make it a mortgage. Loan Amount, Interest Rate and Term.
Although every mortgage needs each of these things to make it a mortgage, it is exactly the exact definition of each of these things

that make it the type of mortgage that one would qualify for and or the type of mortgage one will get.

Each one of these items will also affect other things relating to the mortgage.

Balloon Payment

A balloon payment means that a mortgage note is due in full by a certain date. The reason its called a balloon payment is because even if the mortgage note is due in full by a certain date, the payments are amortized over a longer period. In other words if you have a balloon payment due in 5-10-15 years, your payment could still be based on a 30 year note. So this is what would be considered a 30 due in 15 (30/15). On the 1003 mortgage application in the term section it would look like this 360/180. This represents the months. 360 months (30 years) due in 180 months (15 Years).

When to Refinance

I'm sure you've probably heard it often; another friend or neighbor has refinanced and is enjoying lower monthly mortgage payments. You may have read headlines in the paper or saw in the news about mortgage interest rates reaching historical lows. So, you ask, is now the best time to refinance my mortgage?

Refinancing is essentially paying off your existing mortgage and taking out a new one. In this section you will learn the basics of refinancing, such as the reasons for refinancing and the steps involved.

Over the years, I think this has got to be one of the questions I've probable heard the most. It's a good question and the ones who don't ask are at least thinking of it as they should.

Okay, so lets tackle this one!

When should you refinance?

The answer is, "When it makes sense! What a concept. Simple but true.

The only time anyone and everyone should even consider refinancing is when it makes sense for them.

Each person has a unique and different situation. Some need to save money. Let me rephrase that, everyone could save some money, but some need it more than others. Other homeowners would like do some home improvements by finishing their basement, while some need the money to finish their basement. See the difference in the exact same situation. Would like to and need to!

Others have growing families, want cash out. Maybe their current interest rate is going up? Need to change from FHA to Conventional to get their MIP refund? Can't qualify for anything else, or even need the tax benefits. Need to use the extra savings for investments, savings, loans, etc, etc.

So remember, you should refinance when it makes sense for you! Which also means when it meets your needs. These two things go hand in hand.

But what else does that mean? Is it that simple. Well no, the answer is that simple, but you still need to do your due diligence.

You'll have to do the math for your self.

You'll need to look at the programs.

You'll need to know the companies to look at.

You'll have to know what the closing costs should be, the rate, etc.

You might be asking yourself, "How will I do that"? or "I don't know anything about programs, lenders, brokers, closing costs or rates"?

Don't worry about it! This is why you've purchased this book, and I can honestly promise you that you will understand all of those questions! You can count on that!

I've trained hundreds of sales people over the years, and I can bet you that after reading this book, you'll know more than many people in the industry.

I also train and have trained many, many hundreds of telephone sales representatives that literally in less than one hour are speaking with homeowners about their situations and taking applications with them over the phone.
I've heard on more occasions than I could ever recall from my clients how knowledgeable my telephone representatives are. They're also asked on a regular basis how many years they've been in the business, sometimes even in their first week.

Many of the same telephone representatives I train and work with don't even own a home and actually educate homeowners who've been a homeowner for many years and many who've owned many homes and have had plenty of mortgages over the years.

I'm very proud of this fact to know that my training is not only successful, but that we're helping thousands of homeowners and educating them as well.

On the same note, it saddens me to see so many thousands of homeowners who don't know the basic rules of mortgage industry.
It's a scary thought and is what unscrupulous mortgage professionals count on. Those are the ones that try to make the industry sound harder than it is. These are the lenders and brokers quoting rates, before taking a basic application to see exactly what they can do first, before quoting a rate.

In other words, this book will help you know everything you need to know in order to make an informed educated decision on the most important financial decision you'll most likely make, your mortgage.

Some things you should consider when thinking of refinancing that will help you decide if refinancing is for you and what type of refinancing you should do.

What are you looking for?
Do you want to save money?
Do you want to do home improvements?
What kind of mortgage do you currently have?
What type of rate do you currently have?
How long are you planning on living in that residence?

Chapter II.

Interest Rates

Interest Rates

What are interest rates?

We'll as you all know, mortgage lenders, bankers and brokers lend money or help you get the money in the form of a mortgage (Home Loan). Now I know that most of these lenders and brokers like you and would love to do a mortgage for you for free, but unfortunately they can't. The way lenders and banks make their money is on the interest rates they charge on the mortgages they do.

In other words, as we've covered every mortgage has three things that make it a mortgage. In no particular order, one is the term 10, 15, 20, 25, 30-year mortgage term. Another is the mortgage amount, and last but not least is the interest rate they'll charge on the mortgage amount amortized over the term of the mortgage. All of the interest paid on a mortgage goes to the lender or bank and that's why and how they make their money and is why they lend money.

So as I mentioned before, remember a $200,000 home with a 7.25% fixed interest rate at the average term of 30 years (360 Months) will actually cost the homeowner $488,217.60! So if you subtract the initial mortgage amount of $200,000 from the $488,217.60, the difference would be $288,217.60.

What does that mean you ask? That means that the interest alone paid on the mortgage is $288,217.60 and that amount is based on the 7.25% interest rate.

That's why mortgage lenders and banks lend money. Think about it, they'll make more on the interest than the original amount they lent in the first place. Wow! I wished we all could make more then 100% return on our investments.

So when you hear consumers talking about the interest rates, as you've also probable done, this is why, because you'll spend more on interest than the home itself.

Don't let this number discourage you though. It's a necessary evil. Unless you have $200,000 sitting around in the bank, this is something that's not only worth it, but necessary.

However, this is exactly why you've purchased this book. I'm going to show you ways to save tens of thousands of dollars on interest, regardless of the interest rate and or refinancing.

If you read carefully I mentioned that the interest paid was based on the average term of 30 years (360 Months). SO that means that if you made the exact mortgage payment for the entire 30 years.
We'll even if you don't refinance, you can have huge savings on interest by paying more towards your mortgage principal. You can essentially get an effective interest rate of 1, 2 or even 3 percent or more lower than your actual rate by paying more towards your principal mortgage amount.

This can be done with a bi-weekly payment or even just paying extra on your mortgage principal, but lets not get carried away just yet. We'll be covering all of that in the chapters to come. I just wanted to alleviate some of the tension you we're probable feeling when those numbers were being processed by your mind, and let you know that there are options.

Interest Rate Charts & Points

Okay, this is an important section that you have most likely never known about but have heard of. Many have wondered how interest rates are selected by their mortgage professionals and now I am going to give you a glimpse as to how they get part of their money and also how they select interest rates.

Many mortgage lenders, banks and mortgage professionals in genera have begged me not to include this information in the mortgage book. I have been threatened by some of the giants in the industry all the way down to the mom and pop mortgage companies. I am not telling you this to try to impress you, but to impress upon you the importance of this information and I hope that you apply some of what you learn here and ask the mortgage professionals to show you their rate charts so you can see for yourself what they are making in the back end, yield spread (YSP).

Some of you may have heard of the term back end point, this is where that comes from. Back end points is a yield sprea (YSP) or basis points that lenders will give mortgage professionals in order to use their mortgage products. The lenders will give the mortgage professionals a certain amount of back end points, based on the interest rate they select from their products. It is obvious that the mortgage lenders and banks make their money on the interest payments so they will give the mortgage professionals more back end yield spread or points based on the higher rate they give you the consumer.

So remember, mortgage professionals do have the power to select rates. They can give you a higher or lower rate based on how much more back end points or yield spread (YSP) they would like to earn themselves or their company. Most mortgage professionals are encouraged to give consumers higher rates even if they can give them lower ones for this specific reason. It is a way for the mortgage professional and the company to earn more income or money for not doing anything other than give you a higher rate.
The higher the rate the more of a yield spread (YSP) or back end points they will get.

The yield spread is typically disclosed on the good faith estimate (GFE) on one of the lines that may say YSP or yield spread of 1-3% to broker. So this is another way they earn money and disclose a little bit and it's not in a dollar amount in the good faith estimate because it is not paid in the front, but in the back by the lender.

Lenders that use their own money or fund the mortgage in their name through a warehouse line do not have to disclose this yield spread so depending on what type of mortgage company you use, you may never ever be aware of how much more a mortgage company or professional will get in the back end. This is why you should ask to see the rate sheet. It is quite alright to ask so do not be ashamed to ask. If it is a good deal, the mortgage company and professional will earn a significant amount which is not wrong, but what you want to know is if you are being taken advantage of and being unfairly charged.

Make sense? Do not worry if you are dealing with a mortgage professional is earning a decent level on your loan. I do, and my clients love me for it. Not everyone can afford my fees, but then again not everyone can do what I do! My clients sleep very well at night knowing they are dealing with me.

Keep in mind that professionals in every industry that are the best at what they do all earn good livings on their clients. It is funny how no one questions a brain surgeon if they deserved the $500,000.00 they earned on the brain surgery that took 20 hours? It is also funny how no one questions the attorneys of the rich and famous when they charge millions to keep their clients from loosing a law suit or keep them out of harms way. The list goes on and on. Why doesn't anyone question the professional football player why they get millions per game? Even if they have a bad game? Or the famous movie star that collects $20 plus million per film!

I hope all this is making sense. The bottom line is you should not feel bad if your mortgage professional is earning a decent amount so long as he or she earns it and does not take advantage of you. Part of doing business with the right professional is knowing that although they might earn a descent amount on your mortgage, with the right professional it will still be the very best deal you can get. So this will save you all the time and energy shopping for the right professional, not to mention the fact that you will have peace of mind knowing you are represented by the best!

Enough said, here are some example charts. These are actual charts from one of the many lenders I work with. Keep in mind that these types of charts change on a daily basis and sometimes several times a day. This is only to be used as a training tool and you should pay no attention to the rates and points. Each lender has their own set of rules and back end points they give. Also these were based on today's market rates and will most inevitable change by the time you read this. These charts are also bits and pieces from the original charts. I cannot include the full price sheets. That information is proprietor information. I do however intend to include that and much more in future editions of the mortgage book.

In this example you can see an actual price and rate sheet for a 30 year fixed conventional conforming mortgage and right next to it you can see the same fixed conventional conforming mortgage but the second example which is attached is based on a 15 year. So the box to the left is for 30 years and the box to the right is for 15 years.

Conventional									
C30		30 Year Fixed			**C15**		15 Year Fixed		
Rate	**15 Day**	**30 Day**	**45 Day**	**60 Day**	**Rate**	**15 Day**	**30 Day**	**45 Day**	**60 Day**
5.750%	1.560	1.750	1.825	1.895	5.125%	0.710	0.900	0.975	1.045
5.875%	0.760	0.950	1.025	1.095	5.250%	0.310	0.500	0.575	0.645
6.000%	0.160	0.350	0.425	0.495	5.375%	(0.290)	(0.100)	(0.025)	0.045
6.125%	(0.440)	(0.250)	(0.175)	(0.105)	5.500%	(0.690)	(0.500)	(0.425)	(0.355)
6.250%	(0.940)	(0.750)	(0.675)	(0.605)	5.625%	(1.140)	(0.950)	(0.875)	(0.805)
6.375%	(1.740)	(1.550)	(1.475)	(1.405)	5.750%	(1.740)	(1.550)	(1.475)	(1.405)
6.500%	(2.140)	(1.950)	(1.875)	(1.805)	5.875%	(2.240)	(2.050)	(1.975)	(1.905)
6.625%	(2.540)	(2.350)	(2.275)	(2.205)	6.000%	(2.540)	(2.350)	(2.275)	(2.205)
6.750%	(3.240)	(3.050)	(2.975)	(2.905)	6.125%	(2.940)	(2.750)	(2.675)	(2.605)
6.875%	(3.375)	(3.375)	(3.375)	(3.305)	6.250%	(3.375)	(3.375)	(3.375)	(3.305)

Let me explain what you are looking at. Essentially on the 30 year fixed which is the example to the left, those are all the rates for the day that the mortgage professional can select from.

On the C30 please notice that the interest rate starts at 5.75%. Right next to the interest rate of 5.75% you will find a column that says 15 day. That means on a 15 day lock. In that scenario, that rate of 5.75% locked for 15 days would actually cost 1.56% of the loan amount in order to get it.

Not all rates pay, some rates actually cost. That cost for the rate of 5.75% would be called a discount point. So yes, in a lot of cases when you would like to buy a rate down, you would buy it down in the form of a discount point.

So if you'll notice, all of the rates that have a number figure by it that is not in parenthesis is actually a cost for that rate. Also note that with each increase of the lock period, the rate will cost more or pay more. That is why it is important to make sure you are working with a mortgage professional that knows what he or she is doing because if they don't, they might lock it for a certain lock period that is not realistic for the type of program or situation.

A mortgage professional don't just know his or her ability, but also know the abilities of the companies they work with as well.

For instance, I know several lenders I work with have a slow turn around time. One in particular has a 5 day underwriting turn around time. I don't care how much business I have done or do with them, it is what it is. They will not get it to me any sooner. In reality, there policy is a 5 day underwriting time, but I really don't hear an answer from them for at least 10 days!

Some of you might be thinking, why would I use them?

The answer is very simple. It is because I am a professional and know what I am doing, also the simple fact that they have one of the best interest only programs available and they will close them.

I have other lenders that have a 24 hour underwriting turn around time that I wouldn't use if they were the last lender around.

Once again, some of you are wondering why I wouldn't use them? The same answer applies, because I know what I am doing. Also because 8 out of 10 mortgages they approve do not close and for the ones that don't close, they put my clients through their paces asking for so many things that are not necessary.

So quality and service is not just time, but knowing something is going to happen instead of uncertainty.

The following chart will be on FHA's.
The side box on the left is an FHA 15 year fixed and the box to the right of it is an FHA 1/1, meaning 1 year adjustable rate.

Government									
F15	15 Year Fixed				**FHA ARM 225**				1 Yr. ARM
Rate	**15 Day**	**30 Day**	**45 Day**	**60 Day**	**Rate**	**15 Day**	**30 Day**	**45 Day**	**60 Day**
5.000%	1.385	1.450	1.525	1.595	4.000%	1.720	1.735	1.750	1.765
5.500%	(0.665)	(0.600)	(0.525)	(0.455)	4.250%	0.470	0.485	0.500	0.515
6.000%	(2.615)	(2.550)	(2.475)	(2.405)	4.500%	0.220	0.235	0.250	0.265
6.500%	(3.375)	(3.375)	(3.375)	(3.305)	4.750%	(0.030)	(0.015)	0.000	0.015
					5.000%	(0.380)	(0.365)	(0.350)	(0.335)
FBD	30 Year Buydown								
Rate	**15 Day**	**30 Day**	**45 Day**	**60 Day**					
6.500%	(2.965)	(2.900)	(2.825)	(2.755)					
6.750%	(3.215)	(3.150)	(3.075)	(3.005)					
6.875%	(3.365)	(3.300)	(3.225)	(3.155)					
7.000%	(3.375)	(3.375)	(3.375)	(3.305)					

This next example is on the conventional conforming 3/1 ARM. This means it conforms to government guidelines and is a conventional mortgage. The 3/1 means that it is fixed for 3 years and then can adjust upward or downward after that. This is a strong program and is one I would recommend most of my clients that will maximize their savings on a refinance.

| UPNC31 | | | 3/1 Conforming ARM | |
Rate	15 day	30 day	45 day	60 day
4.250%	0.625	0.750	0.875	1.125
4.375%	0.375	0.500	0.625	0.875
4.500%	0.250	0.375	0.500	0.750
4.625%	0.125	0.250	0.375	0.625
4.750%	0.000	0.125	0.250	0.500
4.875%	(0.125)	0.000	0.125	0.375
5.000%	(0.250)	(0.125)	0.000	0.250
5.125%	(0.250)	(0.125)	0.000	0.250
5.250%	(0.375)	(0.250)	(0.125)	0.125

Max price after adjustment
100.750

The next chart is the exact same as the previous example instead of the 5/1 being fixed for 3 years this one is a 5/1 meaning it is fixed and guaranteed for the first 5 years then it can adjust upward or downward based on the market after the initial 5 years.

UPC51			5/1 Conforming ARM	
Rate	**15 day**	**30 day**	**45 day**	**60 day**
5.375%	0.125	0.250	0.375	0.625
5.500%	(0.125)	0.000	0.125	0.375
5.625%	(0.250)	(0.125)	0.000	0.250
5.750%	(0.500)	(0.375)	(0.250)	0.000
5.875%	(0.750)	(0.625)	(0.500)	(0.250)
6.000%	(0.875)	(0.750)	(0.625)	(0.375)
6.125%	(1.000)	(0.875)	(0.750)	(0.500)

**Max price
after adjustment
100.750**

I hope these charts helped. If they don't make much sense at first, don't feel bad. I know many mortgage professionals that don't know how to read the same exact charts. If they don't make much sense now, try and go over them again.

Keep in mind that all mortgage rates are this way. Not all mortgage companies disclose this to their workers so don't be surprised if you might have to educate some professionals yourself when you call. How ever if you do need to educate a mortgage professional on this topic or any of these topics, know that you are talking to the wrong persona and definitely do not want to work with that person or company.

This book should not make you better or smarter than mortgage professionals, it is supposed to educate you to know what you need and want and then give you the basic knowledge on how to get it using your newly found knowledge. You really still want to work with an industry expert, such as myself. If I'm not available, then work with another industry expert that indeed knows more than you. It is the only way to be 100% safe and know you will get the right mortgage for you with no surprises or horror stories.

Types of Interest Rates

There are many types of interest rates and it can be a little confusing to say the least about the many different types of interest rates. This becomes even more complicated, because some rates are based on types of mortgage programs.
Even when communicating with a mortgage professional, it can be confusing, because the interest rate and the mortgage program are tied together in many cases.

So this is where it gets a little confusing. Interest rates are tied to the different types of mortgages, but not always. In other words, some conventional mortgage interest rates are similar to the FHA mortgage rates.

As for the interest rate itself, the interest rate on conforming mortgages should be very similar. In other words if you get a 7.00% fixed conventional mortgage rate you should be able to get a 7.00% fixed FHA mortgage rate.
Please keep in mind that this is not always the case. Each one of those programs are different bond programs so the actual rates will be determined by the bond trades for each program on the bond market. Lenders and brokers will typically honor or get you the similar rates since they know that the mortgage shoppers have done their research and know what an FHA interest rate would be or vise versa. It would be easier to get a mortgage for someone and get them what rate they're expecting if they're educated with the current rates. It's easier to keep a client and earn less money than to find a whole new client.

Interest rates are different not only with the types of programs and rates themselves, but also in the kind of rate. For instance, you've heard me mention a few times already "fixed rate". I'm always very specific when it comes to interest rates, and I always make sure my clients not only hear me but also understand.

This is an area where many mistakes are made by both the mortgage professionals and the consumers as well. It goes both ways.

Some mortgage professionals don't tell you about the Adjustable Rate Mortgage also known as the arm. Some tell you, but they know you either didn't hear it and or didn't cover it enough. Some mortgage professionals might not have paid enough attention to the consumer to even identify if they heard it or not, or understand it or not.

On the other hand, some consumers don't pay enough attention when the mortgage professionals tell them this is an adjustable rate mortgage (ARM). Some consumers also just want to move on and not hear about it even when a mortgage professional tries to explain in more detail.

So as I mentioned, this is an area that's a problem but it goes both ways, tith the mortgage professional and consumers alike.

Getting back to interest rates, there are many different kinds of rates so its very important to not only know what your interest rate is, but also the type of rate and of course the type of program, which may be directly affecting the kind of interest rate you get.

Fixed Rate

There is the fixed interest rate. The fixed interest rate means that this rate will not change or adjust in any way shape or form for the entire term of the mortgage.

So if you had a 30 year mortgage, and you never ever refinanced, that interest rate would stay the same for the entire 30 years.

There are the adjustable rate mortgages also known as the ARM. With an adjustable rate mortgage the interest rate can adjust upward or downward depending on the bond market and the trading of the particular mortgage you might be in.

There are many different types of adjustable rate mortgages as well, which we'll be covering in more detail in a moment.

Typically when the bond market is up, rates are lower and when the bond market is down the rates are up.

Don't worry about that too much. That's more for the professionals to know. To this day, I don't care what the bond market is doing. It matters not too me if the bond markets up or down, since I don't sell interest rates. I sell the best situation for my clients and sometimes they should stay exactly where they're at if I can't help them save money or put them into a mortgage.

You should also use this same philosophy. It shouldn't matter to you what the bond market is doing. You should only worry about being in a better situation or not. In other words is this a benefit to you and are you saving money? If it's a better situation for you and gives you the savings or meets your needs, then you shouldn't worry about the bond market!

When you have an adjustable rate mortgage, you should worry if the market is up or down when its time for your rate to adjust. Remember if the market is up then the rates are typically down, if the market is down then the rates are up. The only reason you'd want to know when you're rate is scheduled to adjust is because you'd want to know if your rate might be going up, or dropping and also if you might need to refinance or not to avoid a worse situation.

1/1 ARM

Now there are many different types of adjustable rate mortgages. For instance, there is the typical 1/1 ARM. This type of adjustable is available with conventional and FHA mortgages alike, but is not available with VA mortgages.
The 1/1 means that the rate is fixed for a period of 1 year and then can typically adjust upward or downward by 1 percent. The adjustment intervals are also by 1 year, so after the first year, then it takes another

whole year to adjust either way again. In some cases it can adjust a little more than 1 percent, but I've personally never seen that happen with a conforming mortgage.

The 1/1 ARM is the only ARM product available for FHA mortgages.

3/1, 5/1, 7/1, 10/1 ARM's

As with the 1/1 these ARM's are fixed for a period of 3, 5, 7 or 10 year periods then can adjust upward or downward based on the market.

For example, if I gave you a 3/1 ARM, this would mean that your interest rate would be fixed for a period of 3 years, then can adjust upward or downward based on the market after the initial 3 year fixed period. And the same goes for the 5/1, 7/1 and 10/1's.

These kinds of adjustable rate mortgages are currently only available for conventional mortgages and are not available for FHA and VA mortgages. VA mortgages at this moment in time have no kind of adjustable rate. All VA mortgages are fixed.

ARM Vs. Fixed

This is something that most consumers ponder! It's a great question and unfortunately it has been beaten into most consumers that they must have a fixed mortgage. Most consumers have been taught this by their friends, family, co-workers, neighbors, etc.

First of all, in most cases this is the wrong way to look at this. Also, this advise is typically given from someone that has had or has a mortgage and that's the extent of their knowledge in the industry. What a shame that maybe they made a wrong choice in their mortgage selection and now they might be passing that bad advice to someone else. Remember you should be looking out for your best interest and a fixed rate isn't always in your best interest as far as savings go.

Don't get me wrong, I'm not saying that all fixed rate mortgages are bad, I'm not saying that the ARM is the way to go. I'm just trying to point out that most people might have a preconceived notion regarding the ARM's and might make the wrong decision if they don't understand it. Keep an open mind and do what's best for you, even when you hear things from others that might affect the way you look at it.

I truly don't mind either way. I place my clients in the best situation for them and I can do any mortgage under the sun, so I truly don't sell one type of interest rate over another, other than for the simple reason that the interest rate I get my clients are the best for them.

Lets now look at what the difference is between a fixed interest rate and an ARM other than the fact that one is fixed and the other is not.

Why would anyone get an ARM, well the answer is simple. Arms are typically lower than the fixed interest rates.

How much lower are the ARM's over the fixed rates?

That's a great question, and that will depend on the types of ARM's. That's where the 1/1, 3/1, 5/1, 7/1, 10/1 comes into play.

The 1/1 will usually be the lowest possible interest rate, and then it goes up from there. So the 1/1 should be a lower interest rate than the 3/1. The 3/1 should be a lower interest rate than a 5/1, and the 5/1 should be lower than the 7/1. Get the picture.
This is not a rule of thumb though. These rates are based on the bond market, so at times the 5/1 might be trading better than the 1/1 and might be very similar in rate. The 5/1 and 3/1 might be the same or in rare instances the 5/1 might be lower than the 3/1. It's rare, but I have seen it happen. In some situations the fixed rate might be even with a 3/1 or 5/1 and in those cases it would be obvious that you would want to go with the fixed rate in those circumstances.

Most consumers jump at getting a fixed rate. What a mistake. Most say I'll be in this house for the next 10 years, so why get an adjustable. Then before you know it, they've refinanced 3-4 times within the first 5 years alone! So that means that they may have lost thousands of dollars in extra savings because there payments would have been lower with the ARM's. It is unlikely that their rate would have adjusted either way during that short period of time.

From my experience, the average homeowner will refinance on average once every two three years! So when I know what the facts are, I'm mostly looking at doing 3/1 and 5/1's for many of my clients and they love me for it. Especially when I explain it to them first. Believe me, I get resistance from almost all of my clients initially. Then I start showing them the extra money they've lost from their last refinance 1-2 years ago and I always ask if the last mortgage professional even mentioned the ARM. They'll usually answer with a no. Then I say, "what a shame, had I met with you originally, I would have saved you an extra $$", whatever the dollar amount is. I always mention that, and then I say you probable would have told me the same thing last year, when you refinanced. Then I'll look at the credit report and show them that within the last however many years, they've refinanced this many times.
That's usually when it starts to click and make sense. Then I point out that each time, they lost the extra savings with an ARM.

There are those that have purchased their first home and they say, well this is our first home and we haven't refinanced yet. Then I'll point out, well, this is your first home and you're already looking at refinancing 1 year later! They just lost the extra savings from an ARM over the past year.

Now, this isn't a rule of thumb, as I've mentioned. In some situations this doesn't apply, but I'll have to tell you. It's not as often as you'd imagine.

Negotiation the Interest Rates

This is one of the most important reasons homeowners refinance. Well the real reason and bottom line is savings, but savings will typically disguise itself in the form of interest rates.

I've included a section in Chapter XI "Getting the mortgage you want" which goes over everything you need to know to negotiate the interest rate you want and deserve. I have also included proven scripts that will work to get you the mortgage and rate you want and desire. Keep in mind that this is based on reality, so it will get you the best rate and mortgage for your situation and like I have mentioned through out this book. There are qualifying guidelines that you must meet first. Based on that, you will have the ability to get the best mortgage, rates and closing costs based on what you can qualify for.

Please see Chapter XI "Getting the mortgage you want" to learn how to negotiate the right rate and mortgage for you.

Amortization Mortgage Payments

Amortization is the paying down of principal balance over the course (Term) of the loan. In other words, its paying down a $100,000 mortgage over a thirty year term, so the payments are amortized over lets say 30 years.
I'll be including a chart of amortized payments for you to look at and get an idea of some mortgage amounts and payments.

I wish I could just give you a quick calculation for you to be able to work out, but its not a simple calculation and I'd be afraid that you'd get more confused and frustrated trying to do the calculations and might not end up with the right figures anyway.

Be very careful as to whom you listen to regarding these P&I (Principal & Interest) payments. Believe it or not, I've read in other mortgage books some very crazy calculations that aren't always accurate. I'm not going to perpetuate the situation of these horrible wrong calculations and add to the problem. But believe me, I can't believe some of the stuff I've heard and read over the years from so called professionals! It's no shock to see how so many homeowners end up in bad situations with some of these so called professionals are out there.

Don't let that scare you. There are bad professionals in every industry and this is why its so important to educate yourself so you can avoid these situations.

Mortgage Payments / Amortization Chart

The amortization chart is to help you see what your payments would be for certain loan amounts, interest rates and term. This is being provided to help give you an idea on mortgage payments.

30 year (360 Months) at 5.00%

30 Year (360 Months) at 5.25%

Amount	P & I Payment	Amount	P & I Payment
50,000	267.3	50,000	274.90
55,000	294.03	55,000	302.39
60,000	320.76	60,000	329.88
65,000	347.49	65,000	357.37
70,000	374.22	70,000	384.86
75,000	400.95	75,000	412.35
80,000	427.95	80,000	439.84
85,000	454.41	85,000	467.33
90,000	481.13	90,000	494.82
95,000	507.86	95,000	522.31
100,000	534.59	100,000	549.80
105,000	561.32	105,000	577.29
110,000	588.05	110,000	604.78
115,000	614.78	115,000	632.27
120,000	641.51	120,000	659.76

Mortgage Payments / Amortization Chart continued.

30 year (360 Months) at 5.00%

30 Year (360 Months) at 5.25%

Amount	P & I Payment	Amount	P & I Payment
125,000	668.24	125,000	687.25
130,000	694.97	130,000	714.74
135,000	721.70	135,000	742.23
140,000	748.43	140,000	769.72
145,000	775.16	145,000	797.21
150,000	801.89	150,000	824.70
155,000	828.62	155,000	852.19
160,000	855.35	160,000	879.68
165,000	882.08	165,000	907.17
170,000	908.81	170,000	934.66
175,000	935.54	175,000	962.15
180,000	962.27	180,000	989.64
185,000	989.00	185,000	1,017.13
190,000	1,015.73	190,000	1,044.62
195,000	1,042.46	195,000	1,072.11
200,000	1,069.19	200,000	1,099.60
205,000	1,095.92	205,000	1,127.09
210,000	1,122.65	210,000	1,154.58
215,000	1,149.38	215,000	1,182.07
220,000	1,176.11	220,000	1,209.56
225,000	1,202.84	225,000	1,237.05
230,000	1,229.57	230,000	1,264.54
235,000	1,256.30	235,000	1,292.03
240,000	1,283.03	240,000	1,319.52
245,000	1,309.76	245,000	1,347.01
250,000	1,336.49	250,000	1,374.50

30 year (360 Months) at 5.50%

30 Year (360 Months) at 5.75%

Amount	P & I Payment	Amount	P & I Payment
50,000	282.60	50,000	290.39
55,000	310.86	55,000	319.43
60,000	339.12	60,000	348.47
65,000	367.38	65,000	377.51
70,000	395.64	70,000	406.55
75,000	423.90	75,000	435.59
80,000	452.16	80,000	464.63
85,000	480.42	85,000	493.67
90,000	508.68	90,000	522.71
95,000	536.94	95,000	551.75
100,000	565.20	100,000	580.79
105,000	593.46	105,000	609.83
110,000	621.72	110,000	638.87
115,000	649.98	115,000	667.91
120,000	678.24	120,000	696.95
125,000	706.50	125,000	725.99
130,000	734.76	130,000	755.03
135,000	763.02	135,000	784.07
140,000	791.28	140,000	813.11
145,000	819.54	145,000	842.15
150,000	847.80	150,000	871.18
155,000	876.06	155,000	900.22
160,000	904.32	160,000	929.26
165,000	932.58	165,000	958.30
170,000	960.84	170,000	987.34
175,000	989.10	175,000	1,016.38
180,000	1,017.36	180,000	1,045.42
185,000	1,045.62	185,000	1,074.46
190,000	1,017.88	190,000	1,103.50
195,000	1,102.14	195,000	1,132.54
200,000	1,130.40	200,000	1,161.58
205,000	1,158.66	205,000	1,190.62

Mortgage Payments / Amortization Chart continued.

30 year (360 Months) at 5.50%		30 Year (360 Months) at 5.75%	
Amount	P & I Payment	Amount	P & I Payment
210,000	1,186.92	210,000	1,219.66
215,000	1,215.18	215,000	1,248.70
220,000	1,243.44	220,000	1,277.74
225,000	1,271.70	225,000	1,306.78
230,000	1,299.96	230,000	1,335.82
235,000	1,328.22	235,000	1,364.86
240,000	1,356.48	240,000	1,393.90
245,000	1,384.74	245,000	1,422.94
250,000	1,413.00	250,000	1,451.97

30 year (360 Months) at 6.00%		30 Year (360 Months) at 6.25%	
Amount	P & I Payment	Amount	P & I Payment
50,000	298.28	50,000	306.26
55,000	328.11	55,000	336.89
60,000	357.94	60,000	367.52
65,000	387.77	65,000	398.14
70,000	417.60	70,000	428.77
75,000	447.43	75,000	459.40
80,000	477.25	80,000	490.02
85,000	507.08	85,000	520.65
90,000	536.91	90,000	551.27
95,000	566.74	95,000	581.90
100,000	596.57	100,000	612.53
105,000	626.40	105,000	643.15
110,000	656.22	110,000	673.78
115,000	686.05	115,000	704.41
120,000	715.88	120,000	735.03

Mortgage Payments / Amortization Chart continued.

30 year (360 Months) at 6.00%

30 Year (360 Months) at 6.25%

Amount	P & I Payment	Amount	P & I Payment
125,000	745.71	125,000	765.66
130,000	775.54	130,000	796.29
135,000	805.37	135,000	826.91
140,000	835.19	140,000	857.54
145,000	865.02	145,000	888.16
150,000	894.85	150,000	918.79
155,000	924.68	155,000	949.42
160,000	954.51	160,000	980.04
165,000	984.34	165,000	1,010.67
170,000	1,014.17	170,000	1,041.30
175,000	1,043.99	175,000	1,071.92
180,000	1,073.82	180,000	1,102.55
185,000	1,103.65	185,000	1,133.17
190,000	1,133.48	190,000	1,163.80
195,000	1,163.31	195,000	1,194.43
200,000	1,193.14	200,000	1,225.05
205,000	1,222.96	205,000	1,255.68
210,000	1,252.79	210,000	1,286.31
215,000	1,282.62	215,000	1,316.93
220,000	1,312.45	220,000	1,347.56
225,000	1,342.28	225,000	1,378.19
230,000	1,372.11	230,000	1,408.81
235,000	1,401.93	235,000	1,433.44
240,000	1,431.76	240,000	1,470.06
245,000	1,461.59	245,000	1,500.69
250,000	1,491.42	250,000	1,531.32

30 year (360 Months) at 6.50%		30 Year (360 Months) at 6.75%	
Amount	P & I Payment	Amount	P & I Payment
50,000	314.33	50,000	322.49
55,000	345.76	55,000	354.73
60,000	377.20	60,000	386.98
65,000	408.63	65,000	419.23
70,000	440.06	70,000	451.48
75,000	471.50	75,000	483.73
80,000	502.93	80,000	515.98
85,000	534.36	85,000	548.22
90,000	565.80	90,000	580.47
95,000	597.23	95,000	612.72
100,000	628.66	100,000	644.97
105,000	660.10	105,000	677.22
110,000	691.53	110,000	709.47
115,000	722.96	115,000	741.72
120,000	754.40	120,000	773.96
125,000	785.83	125,000	806.21
130,000	817.26	130,000	838.46
135,000	848.69	135,000	870.71
140,000	880.13	140,000	902.96
145,000	911.56	145,000	935.21
150,000	942.99	150,000	967.46
155,000	974.43	155,000	999.70
160,000	1,005.86	160,000	1,031.95
165,000	1,037.29	165,000	1,064.20
170,000	1,068.73	170,000	1,096.45
175,000	1,100.16	175,000	1,128.70
180,000	1,131.59	180,000	1,160.95
185,000	1,163.03	185,000	1,193.19
190,000	1,194.46	190,000	1,225.44
195,000	1,225.89	195,000	1,257.69
200,000	1,257.33	200,000	1,289.94
205,000	1,288.76	205,000	1,322.19
210,000	1,320.19	210,000	1,354.44

Mortgage Payments / Amortization Chart continued.

30 year (360 Months)
at 6.50%

Amount	P & I Payment
215,000	1,351.62
220,000	1,383.06
225,000	1,414.49
230,000	1,445.92
235,000	1,477.36
240,000	1,508.79
245,000	1,540.22
250,000	1,571.66

30 Year (360 Months)
at 6.75%

Amount	P & I Payment
215,000	1,386.69
220,000	1,418.93
225,000	1,451.18
230,000	1,483.43
235,000	1,515.68
240,000	1,547.93
245,000	1,580.18
250,000	1,612.43

30 year (360 Months)
at 7.00%

Amount	P & I Payment
50,000	330.72
55,000	363.79
60,000	396.87
65,000	429.94
70,000	463.01
75,000	496.08
80,000	529.16
85,000	562.23
90,000	595.30
95,000	628.37
100,000	661.44
105,000	694.52
110,000	727.59
115,000	760.66
120,000	793.73
125,000	826.81
130,000	859.88

30 Year (360 Months)
at 7.25%

Amount	P & I Payment
50,000	339.04
55,000	372.94
60,000	406.85
65,000	440.75
70,000	474.66
75,000	508.56
80,000	542.46
85,000	576.37
90,000	610.27
95,000	644.18
100,000	678.08
105,000	711.98
110,000	745.89
115,000	779.79
120,000	813.70
125,000	847.60
130,000	881.50

Mortgage Payments / Amortization Chart continued.

30 year (360 Months) at 7.00%		30 Year (360 Months) at 7.25%	
Amount	P & I Payment	Amount	P & I Payment
135,000	892.95	135,000	915.41
140,000	926.02	140,000	949.31
145,000	959.09	145,000	983.22
150,000	992.17	150,000	1,017.12
155,000	1,025.24	155,000	1,051.02
160,000	1,058.31	160,000	1,089.93
165,000	1,091.38	165,000	1,118.83
170,000	1,124.45	170,000	1,152.74
175,000	1,157.53	175,000	1,186.64
180,000	1,190.60	180,000	1,220.54
185,000	1,223.67	185,000	1,254.45
190,000	1,256.74	190,000	1,288.35
195,000	1,289.82	195,000	1,322.26
200,000	1,322.89	200,000	1,356.16
205,000	1,355.96	205,000	1,390.06
210,000	1,389.03	210,000	1,423.97
215,000	1,422.10	215,000	1,457.87
220,000	1,455.18	220,000	1,491.78
225,000	1,488.25	225,000	1,525.68
230,000	1,521.32	230,000	1,559.58
235,000	1,554.39	235,000	1,593.49
240,000	1,587.47	240,000	1,627.39
245,000	1,620.54	245,000	1,661.29
250,000	1,653.61	250,000	1,695.20

30 year (360 Months)
at 7.50%

30 Year (360 Months)
at 7.75%

Amount	P & I Payment	Amount	P & I Payment
50,000	347.44	50,000	355.91
55,000	382.18	55,000	391.50
60,000	416.92	60,000	427.09
65,000	451.67	65,000	462.68
70,000	486.41	70,000	498.27
75,000	521.15	75,000	533.86
80,000	555.90	80,000	569.45
85,000	590.64	85,000	605.04
90,000	625.38	90,000	640.63
95,000	660.13	95,000	676.22
100,000	694.87	100,000	711.82
105,000	729.62	105,000	747.41
110,000	764.36	110,000	783.00
115,000	799.10	115,000	818.59
120,000	833.85	120,000	854.18
125,000	868.59	125,000	889.77
130,000	903.33	130,000	925.36
135,000	938.08	135,000	960.95
140,000	972.83	140,000	996.54
145,000	1,007.56	145,000	1,032.13
150,000	1,042.31	150,000	1,067.72
155,000	1,077.05	155,000	1,103.31
160,000	1,111.79	160,000	1,138.90
165,000	1,146.54	165,000	1,174.49
170,000	1,181.28	170,000	1,174.49
175,000	1,216.03	175,000	1,245.68
180,000	1,250.77	180,000	1,281.27
185,000	1,285.51	185,000	1,316.86
190,000	1,320.26	190,000	1,352.45
195,000	1,355.00	195,000	1,388.04
200,000	1,389.74	200,000	1,423.63
205,000	1,424.49	205,000	1,459.22

Mortgage Payments / Amortization Chart continued.

30 year (360 Months) at 7.50%			30 Year (360 Months) at 7.75%	
Amount	P & I Payment		Amount	P & I Payment
210,000	1,459.23		210,000	1,494.81
215,000	1,493.97		215,000	1,530.40
220,000	1,528.72		220,000	1,565.99
225,000	1,563.46		225,000	1,601.58
230,000	1,598.20		230,000	1,637.17
235,000	1,632.95		235,000	1,627.77
240,000	1,667.69		240,000	1,708.36
245,000	1,702.44		245,000	1,743.95
250,000	1,737.18		250,000	1,779.54

30 year (360 Months) at 8.00%			30 Year (360 Months) at 8.25%	
Amount	P & I Payment		Amount	P & I Payment
50,000	364.45		50,000	373.07
55,000	400.90		55,000	410.38
60,000	437.34		60,000	447.68
65,000	473.79		65,000	484.99
70,000	510.23		70,000	522.30
75,000	546.68		75,000	559.60
80,000	583.12		80,000	596.91
85,000	619.57		85,000	634.22
90,000	656.01		90,000	671.52
95,000	692.46		95,000	708.83
100,000	728.91		100,000	746.14
105,000	765.35		105,000	783.44
110,000	801.80		110,000	820.75
115,000	838.24		115,000	858.06
120,000	874.69		120,000	895.36

Mortgage Payments / Amortization Chart continued.

30 year (360 Months) at 8.00%		30 Year (360 Months) at 8.25%	
Amount	P & I Payment	Amount	P & I Payment
125,000	911.13	125,000	932.67
130,000	947.58	130,000	969.98
135,000	984.02	135,000	1,007.28
140,000	1,020.47	140,000	1,044.59
145,000	1,056.91	145,000	1,089.90
150,000	1,093.36	150,000	1,119.21
155,000	1,129.80	155,000	1,156.51
160,000	1,166.25	160,000	1,193.82
165,000	1,202.69	165,000	1,231.13
170,000	1,239.14	170,000	1,268.43
175,000	1,275.58	175,000	1,305.74
180,000	1,312.03	180,000	1,343.05
185,000	1,348.47	185,000	1,380.35
190,000	1,384.92	190,000	1,417.66
195,000	1,421.37	195,000	1,454.97
200,000	1,457.81	200,000	1,492.27
205,000	1,494.26	205,000	1,529.58
210,000	1,530.70	210,000	1,566.89
215,000	1,567.15	215,000	1,604.19
220,000	1,603.59	220,000	1,641.50
225,000	1,640.04	225,000	1,678.81
230,000	1,676.48	230,000	1,716.11
235,000	1,712.93	235,000	1,753.42
240,000	1,749.37	240,000	1,790.73
245,000	1,785.82	245,000	1,828.04
250,000	1,822.26	250,000	1,865.34

Mortgage Payments / Amortization Chart

The amortization chart is to help you see what your payments would be for certain loan amounts, interest rates and term. This is being provided to help give you an idea on mortgage payments.

15 year (180 Months) at 4.00%		15 Year (180 Months) at 4.25%	
Amount	P & I Payment	Amount	P & I Payment
50,000	368.62	50,000	374.81
55,000	405.48	55,000	412.29
60,000	442.34	60,000	449.77
65,000	479.20	65,000	487.26
70,000	516.06	70,000	524.74
75,000	552.92	75,000	562.22
80,000	589.78	80,000	599.70
85,000	626.65	85,000	637.18
90,000	663.51	90,000	674.66
95,000	700.37	95,000	712.14
100,000	737.23	100,000	749.62
105,000	774.09	105,000	787.10
110,000	810.95	110,000	824.59
115,000	847.82	115,000	862.07
120,000	884.68	120,000	899.55
125,000	921.54	125,000	937.03
130,000	958.40	130,000	974.51
135,000	995.26	135,000	1,011.99
140,000	1,032.12	140,000	1,049.47
145,000	1,068.98	145,000	1,086.95
150,000	1,105.85	150,000	1,124.44
155,000	1,142.71	155,000	1,161.92
160,000	1,179.57	160,000	1,199.40
165,000	1,216.43	165,000	1,236.88
170,000	1,253.29	170,000	1,274.36
175,000	1,290.15	175,000	1,311.84

Mortgage Payments / Amortization Chart continued.

15 year (180 Months)
at 4.00%

Amount Payment	P & I Payment
180,000	1,327.01
185,000	1,363.88
190,000	1,400.74
195,000	1,437.60
200,000	1,474.46
205,000	1,511.32
210,000	1,548.18
215,000	1,585.05
220,000	1,621.91
225,000	1,658.77
230,000	1,695.63
235,000	1,732.49
240,000	1,769.35
245,000	1,806.21
250,000	1,843.08

15 Year (180 Months)
at 4.25%

Amount	P & I
180,000	1,349.32
185,000	1,386.80
190,000	1,424.28
195,000	1,461.77
200,000	1,499.25
205,000	1,536.73
210,000	1,574.21
215,000	1,611.69
220,000	1,649.17
225,000	1,686.65
230,000	1,724.13
235,000	1,761.62
240,000	1,799.10
245,000	1,836.58
250,000	1,874.06

15 year (180 Months)
at 4.50%

Amount	P & I Payment
50,000	381.07
55,000	419.17
60,000	457.28
65,000	495.39
70,000	533.49
75,000	571.60
80,000	609.71
85,000	647.81
90,000	685.92

15 Year (180 Months)
at 4.75%

Amount	P & I Payment
50,000	387.38
55,000	426.12
60,000	464.86
65,000	503.60
70,000	542.34
75,000	581.07
80,000	619.81
85,000	658.55
90,000	697.29

Mortgage Payments / Amortization Chart continued.

15 year (180 Months) at 4.50%		15 Year (180 Months) at 4.75%	
Amount	P & I Payment	Amount	P & I Payment
95,000	724.03	95,000	736.03
100,000	762.14	100,000	774.77
105,000	800.24	105,000	813.50
110,000	838.35	110,000	852.24
115,000	876.46	115,000	890.98
120,000	914.56	120,000	929.72
125,000	952.67	125,000	968.46
130,000	990.78	130,000	1,007.19
135,000	1,028.88	135,000	1,045.93
140,000	1,066.99	140,000	1,084.67
145,000	1,105.10	145,000	1,123.41
150,000	1,143.20	150,000	1,162.15
155,000	1,181.31	155,000	1,200.89
160,000	1,219.42	160,000	1,239.62
165,000	1,257.52	165,000	1,278.36
170,000	1,295.63	170,000	1,317.10
175,000	1,333.74	175,000	1,355.84
180,000	1,371.84	180,000	1,394.58
185,000	1,409.95	185,000	1,433.32
190,000	1,448.06	190,000	1,472.05
195,000	1,486.16	195,000	1,510.79
200,000	1,524.27	200,000	1,549.53
205,000	1,562.38	205,000	1,588.27
210,000	1,600.48	210,000	1,627.01
215,000	1,638.59	215,000	1,665.75
220,000	1,676.70	220,000	1,704.48
225,000	1,714.80	225,000	1,743.22
230,000	1,752.91	230,000	1,781.96
235,000	1,791.02	235,000	1,820.70
240,000	1,829.12	240,000	1,859.44

Mortgage Payments / Amortization Chart continued.

15 year (180 Months) at 4.50%

Amount	P & I Payment
245,000	1,867.23
250,000	1,905.34

15 Year (180 Months) at 4.75%

Amount	P & I Payment
245,000	1,898.17
250,000	1,936.91

15 year (180 Months) at 5.00%

Amount	P & I Payment
50,000	393.76
55,000	433.13
60,000	472.51
65,000	511.88
70,000	551.26
75,000	590.63
80,000	630.01
85,000	669.39
90,000	708.76
95,000	748.14
100,000	787.51
105,000	826.89
110,000	866.26
115,000	905.64
120,000	945.01
125,000	984.39
130,000	1,023.77
135,000	1,063.14
140,000	1,102.52
145,000	1,141.89
150,000	1,181.27
155,000	1,220.64

15 Year (180 Months) at 5.25%

Amount	P & I Payment
50,000	400.19
55,000	440.21
60,000	480.23
65,000	520.24
70,000	560.26
75,000	600.28
80,000	640.30
85,000	680.32
90,000	720.34
95,000	760.36
100,000	800.38
105,000	840.39
110,000	880.41
115,000	920.43
120,000	960.45
125,000	1,000.47
130,000	1,040.49
135,000	1,080.51
140,000	1,120.53
145,000	1,160.55
150,000	1,200.56
155,000	1,240.58

Mortgage Payments / Amortization Chart continued.

15 year (180 Months)
at 5.00%

Amount	P & I Payment
160,000	1,260.02
165,000	1,299.40
170,000	1,338.77
175,000	1,378.15
180,000	1,417.52
185,000	1,456.90
190,000	1,496.27
195,000	1,535.65
200,000	1,575.02
205,000	1,614.40
210,000	1,653.78
215,000	1,693.15
220,000	1,732.53
225,000	1,771.90
230,000	1,811.28
235,000	1,850.65
240,000	1,890.03
245,000	1,929.41
250,000	1,968.78

15 Year (180 Months)
at 5.25%

Amount	P & I Payment
160,000	1,280.60
165,000	1,320.62
170,000	1,360.64
175,000	1,400.66
180,000	1,440.68
185,000	1,480.70
190,000	1,520.71
195,000	1,560.73
200,000	1,600.75
205,000	1,640.77
210,000	1,680.79
215,000	1,720.81
220,000	1,760.83
225,000	1,800.85
230,000	1,840.86
235,000	1,880.88
240,000	1,920.90
245,000	1,960.92
250,000	2,000.94

15 year (180 Months)
at 5.50%

Amount	P & I Payment
50,000	406.68
55,000	447.35
60,000	488.01
65,000	528.68
70,000	569.35

15 Year (180 Months)
at 5.75%

Amount	P & I Payment
50,000	413.23
55,000	454.55
60,000	495.87
65,000	537.19
70,000	578.52

Mortgage Payments / Amortization Chart continued.

15 year (180 Months) at 5.50%		15 Year (180 Months) at 5.75%	
Amount	P & I Payment	Amount	P & I Payment
75,000	610.02	75,000	619.84
80,000	650.68	80,000	661.16
85,000	691.35	85,000	702.48
90,000	732.02	90,000	743.81
95,000	772.69	95,000	785.13
100,000	813.36	100,000	826.45
105,000	854.02	105,000	867.77
110,000	894.69	110,000	909.10
115,000	935.36	115,000	950.42
120,000	976.03	120,000	991.74
125,000	1,016.69	125,000	1,033.06
130,000	1,057.36	130,000	1,074.39
135,000	1,098.03	135,000	1,115.71
140,000	1,138.70	140,000	1,157.03
145,000	1,179.37	145,000	1,198.35
150,000	1,220.03	150,000	1,239.68
155,000	1,260.70	155,000	1,281.00
160,000	1,301.37	160,000	1,322.32
165,000	1,342.04	165,000	1,363.64
170,000	1,382.70	170,000	1,404.97
175,000	1,423.37	175,000	1,446.29
180,000	1,464.04	180,000	1,487.61
185,000	1,504.71	185,000	1,528.93
190,000	1,545.38	190,000	1,570.26
195,000	1,586.04	195,000	1,611.58
200,000	1,626.71	200,000	1,652.90
205,000	1,667.38	205,000	1,694.22
210,000	1,708.05	210,000	1,735.55
215,000	1,748.71	215,000	1,776.87
220,000	1,789.38	220,000	1,818.19

Mortgage Payments / Amortization Chart continued.

15 year (180 Months) at 5.50%		15 Year (180 Months) at 5.75%	
Amount	P & I Payment	Amount	P & I Payment
225,000	1,830.05	225,000	1,859.51
230,000	1,870.72	230,000	1,900.84
235,000	1,911.39	235,000	1,942.16
240,000	1,952.05	240,000	1,983.48
245,000	1,992.72	245,000	2,024.80
250,000	2,033.39	250,000	2,066.13

15 year (180 Months) at 6.00%		15 Year (180 Months) at 6.25%	
Amount	P & I Payment	Amount	P & I Payment
50,000	419.83	50,000	426.49
55,000	461.81	55,000	469.14
60,000	503.80	60,000	511.79
65,000	545.78	65,000	554.44
70,000	587.76	70,000	597.09
75,000	629.74	75,000	639.74
80,000	671.73	80,000	682.38
85,000	713.71	85,000	725.03
90,000	755.69	90,000	767.68
95,000	797.68	95,000	810.33
100,000	839.66	100,000	852.98
105,000	881.64	105,000	895.63
110,000	923.62	110,000	938.28
115,000	965.61	115,000	980.93
120,000	1,007.59	120,000	1,023.58
125,000	1,049.57	125,000	1,066.23
130,000	1,091.56	130,000	1,108.87
135,000	1,133.54	135,000	1,151.52

Mortgage Payments / Amortization Chart continued.

15 year (180 Months) at 6.00%		15 Year (180 Months) at 6.25%	
Amount	P & I Payment	Amount	P & I Payment
140,000	1,175.52	140,000	1,194.17
145,000	1,217.50	145,000	1,236.82
150,000	1,259.49	150,000	1,279.47
155,000	1,301.47	155,000	1,322.12
160,000	1,343.45	160,000	1,364.77
165,000	1,385.44	165,000	1,407.42
170,000	1,427.42	170,000	1,450.07
175,000	1,469.40	175,000	1,492.72
180,000	1,511.39	180,000	1,535.36
185,000	1,553.37	185,000	1,578.01
190,000	1,595.35	190,000	1,620.66
195,000	1,637.33	195,000	1,663.31
200,000	1,679.32	200,000	1,705.96
205,000	1,721.30	205,000	1,748.61
210,000	1,763.28	210,000	1,791.26
215,000	1,805.27	215,000	1,833.91
220,000	1,847.25	220,000	1,876.56
225,000	1,889.23	225,000	1,919.21
230,000	1,931.21	230,000	1,961.85
235,000	1,973.20	235,000	2,004.50
240,000	2,015.18	240,000	2,047.15
245,000	2,057.16	245,000	2,089.80
250,000	2,099.15	250,000	2,132.45

Oliver P. Maldonado

15 year (180 Months)
at 6.50%

15 Year (180 Months)
at 6.75%

Amount	P & I Payment	Amount	P & I Payment
50,000	433.21	50,000	439.98
55,000	476.53	55,000	483.98
60,000	519.85	60,000	527.98
65,000	563.17	65,000	571.97
70,000	606.49	70,000	615.97
75,000	649.81	75,000	659.97
80,000	693.13	80,000	703.97
85,000	736.45	85,000	747.97
90,000	779.77	90,000	791.96
95,000	823.09	95,000	835.96
100,000	866.41	100,000	879.96
105,000	909.74	105,000	923.96
110,000	953.06	110,000	967.96
115,000	996.38	115,000	1,011.95
120,000	1,039.70	120,000	1,055.95
125,000	1,089.02	125,000	1,099.95
130,000	1,126.34	130,000	1,143.95
135,000	1,169.66	135,000	1,187.95
140,000	1,212.98	140,000	1,231.94
145,000	1,256.30	145,000	1,275.94
150,000	1,299.62	150,000	1,319.94
155,000	1,342.94	155,000	1,363.94
160,000	1,386.26	160,000	1,407.94
165,000	1,429.58	165,000	1,451.93
170,000	1,472.90	170,000	1,495.93
175,000	1,516.23	175,000	1,539.93
180,000	1,559.55	180,000	1,583.93
185,000	1,602.87	185,000	1,627.93
190,000	1,646.19	190,000	1,671.92
195,000	1,689.51	195,000	1,715.92
200,000	1,732.83	200,000	1,759.92
205,000	1,776.15	205,000	1,803.92

Mortgage Payments / Amortization Chart continued.

15 year (180 Months)
at 6.50%

Amount	P & I Payment
210,000	1,819.47
215,000	1,862.79
220,000	1,906.11
225,000	1,949.43
230,000	1,992.75
235,000	2,036.07
240,000	2,079.39
245,000	2,122.72
250,000	2,166.04

15 Year (180 Months)
at 6.75%

Amount	P & I Payment
210,000	1,847.92
215,000	1,891.91
220,000	1,935.91
225,000	1,979.91
230,000	2,023.91
235,000	2,067.91
240,000	2,111.90
245,000	2,155.90
250,000	2,199.90

15 year (180 Months)
at 7.00%

Amount	P & I Payment
50,000	439.98
55,000	483.98
60,000	527.98
65,000	571.97
70,000	615.97
75,000	659.97
80,000	703.97
85,000	747.97
90,000	791.96
95,000	835.96
100,000	879.96
105,000	923.96
110,000	967.96
115,000	1,011.95
120,000	1,055.95

15 Year (180 Months)
at 7.25%

Amount	P & I Payment
50,000	453.69
55,000	499.06
60,000	544.43
65,000	589.80
70,000	635.17
75,000	680.54
80,000	725.90
85,000	771.27
90,000	816.64
95,000	862.01
100,000	907.38
105,000	952.75
110,000	998.12
115,000	1,043.49
120,000	1,088.86

Mortgage Payments / Amortization Chart continued.

15 year (180 Months) at 7.00%		15 Year (180 Months) at 7.25%	
Amount	P & I Payment	Amount	P & I Payment
125,000	1,099.95	125,000	1,134.23
130,000	1,143.95	130,000	1,179.60
135,000	1,187.95	135,000	1,224.96
140,000	1,231.94	140,000	1,270.33
145,000	1,275.94	145,000	1,315.70
150,000	1,319.94	150,000	1,361.07
155,000	1,363.94	155,000	1,406.44
160,000	1,407.94	160,000	1,451.81
165,000	1,451.93	165,000	1,497.18
170,000	1,495.93	170,000	1,542.55
175,000	1,539.93	175,000	1,587.92
180,000	1,583.93	180,000	1,633.29
185,000	1,627.93	185,000	1,678.65
190,000	1,671.92	190,000	1,724.02
195,000	1,715.92	195,000	1,769.39
200,000	1,759.92	200,000	1,814.76
205,000	1,803.92	205,000	1,860.13
210,000	1,847.92	210,000	1,905.50
215,000	1,891.91	215,000	1,950.87
220,000	1,935.91	220,000	1,996.24
225,000	1,979.91	225,000	2,041.61
230,000	2,023.91	230,000	2,086.98
235,000	2,067.91	235,000	2,132.34
240,000	2,111.90	240,000	2,177.71
245,000	2,155.90	245,000	2,223.08
250,000	2,199.90	250,000	2,268.45

Negotiating the interest rate

Please see the Chapter XI. Getting the mortgage you want.

Chapter III.

Lenders

What is a lender?

Simple put, a lender is a bank or lending institution that will lend you a home loan also known as the mortgage. A lender will typically use their own money to loan, that's what makes them a lender. A lender could also be considered a banker and by definition they are.

That's the easy part.

The hard part is knowing what type of lender they are. Mortgage bankers and Lenders make up only about 20% of all mortgages done. Most or the other 80% of the mortgages are done by brokers or mortgage companies who use the lenders money but aren't necessarily the lenders themselves.
In many cases the lenders will also allow others to use their money but the consumer may not even be aware of it.

Even lenders themselves will typically use other lenders money to fund home loans. A lender will do that if they didn't have the right program available and if it wasn't against their policy to use another lenders money.

As you can see, this is when it starts getting tricky, but don't worry. You don't need to know who's a lender and who's not. What you need to know is what type of lender you're dealing with. We'll be covering that in more detail in the later chapters.

This is a very important topic that can put you into the right situation or can put you into a very bad situation.

Choosing the right lender is very important and what you don't know can hurt you.

What makes a lender?

A lender is an entity that has the ability to loan money. This does not necessarily mean that they loan their own money. In many occasions a lender will borrow money in order to loan the money out. This can also be classified as a broker, but if that lender also loans their own money, they will most likely call themselves a lender.
A lender by definition is also a banker.

When to use a lender?

The answer to this is very simple and follows the same theme that we've used through out this process. You should use a lender the same time and for the same reasons you would use a broker or banker. When it makes sense. If the mortgage makes sense and you feel confident it is the right mortgage for you, then by all means use the mortgage lender or for that matter banker or broker to finalize. There is no real reason to use one form of lending institution versus another so long as they are meeting your needs and putting you into the right situation!

Make sense?

Use what ever means of obtaining the right mortgage for you, once you have educated yourself enough to know what it is you need, qualify for and want.

Types of lenders

Did you know there are several types of mortgage companies (Lenders)?

There are A Lender's (Prime Lenders), B&C Lender's (Sub-Prime Lenders), 2nd Mortgage Lender's (Equity Lenders), Government Lenders (FHA, VA), 125% Lender's (Above home value), so on & so forth.

A Lenders (Prime Lenders / Good Credit)

Some of these lenders specialize in dealing with only the A paper (Good Credit), which means they will not & cannot do a loan for someone with previous credit issues (Bad Credit), they only deal with the A credit borrower.

B & C Lenders (Sub-Prime / Bad Credit)

The B&C (High risk, Sub-Prime) Lender's specialize with the homeowner's (Borrowers) that have previous credit issues such as Bankruptcies, Foreclosures, Late Payments, Charge Offs, Repossession's & the such. Don't let that fool you, though they specialize in those B&C programs they would gladly do a loan for a homeowner that may not need that type of program the only problem is the loan would be at very high interest rates & very high closing fees. In other words, not the right program. These are the horror stories you've probable heard of or even suffered through.

Unfortunately there are some people in this industry that would miss lead a homeowner just to get a sale & would not disclose what type of company they are & who would even go so far as to lie to their clients & explain how that is the only program they would qualify for. That is the best rate on the market. That is most definitely the lowest possible closing fees they can get, etc, etc, etc…

2nd Mortgage lenders (Equity Lenders)

The 2nd mortgage companies deal in most cases with only 2nd mortgages, also known as equity loans. Once again even though they specialize in 2nd mortgages & are not very competitive in 1st mortgages they would be glad to do a high rate, high closing fee 1st mortgage for you. These companies may even just talk you into a 2nd mortgage & leave you with the high rate you already have on your 1st.

Other companies specialize in government mortgages & yep they would also be glad to get you a government loan even though that is not the best loan for your situation. Some companies do not do any government mortgages & that might be exactly what you need, but once again they would lead you in that direction.

WHY WOULD ALL OF THESE COMPANIES LEAD YOU IN THE WRONG DIRECTION?

In most cases it is not because they are bad people it is just how they have been trained, & it is their job. How long do you think they would last with that company if they turned business down, not very long. They would loose their job!

In some cases they just do not know any better. Some companies actually hire people that know nothing about the industry just so they can train them with only one type of mortgage & only one type of situation so they just don't know any better.

In all cases they are giving you the best situation they can get you, so they are not technically lying to you. They just forget to tell you that they are a B&C (high risk) lender & that they only have high rates with high closing fees because they deal with only one type of mortgage, the high risk mortgage.

Watch out! Be careful! Some of the things you need to look for and ask for will follow. I'll try to explain what to look out for and what questions to ask.

First of all, you've all probable seen or heard the ads that say "Need Money? Bad Credit, No Credit, No Problem!"
Watch out for these companies. These are what you would call the sub-prime or bad credit lenders. Not all are bad and some might offer special programs, but by large most are sub-prime or B & C lenders. Although these programs and lenders offer great programs for people with bad credit, these lenders and programs are not meant for someone with good credit! If you have good credit, you'll spend way too much on closing costs and interest with these lenders and programs so beware.

Some of these types of lenders are what would some call predatory lending. Sometimes these lenders would direct borrowers away from loans with more affordable interest rates and closing costs. Instead they would offer you a very high interest rate, high closing costs some of which are questionable at best.

These practices are what are known as predatory.

The A lenders are lenders that deal primarily with good credit borrowers. They offer programs such as FHA, VA, and conventional. This is the type of lender you should really try to deal with even if your credit isn't that good. The worst that would happen to you if you have bad credit is that you'd get turned down and you may loose a few points when they pull your credit, but at least they'd tell you or should tell you the reason why. At least you wouldn't end up with the wrong program.

The good, bad and ugly lenders
The B&C (Sub-Prime)

The large majority of the horror stories that you may have heard or have even experienced come from these types of lenders. The B&C or Sub-Prime lenders. Just look at the name, B&C lenders. What do you think that's referring to? As you've heard already there is A credit and B & C credit! The A credit is the good credit. The B & C credit is the bad credit.

These are the lenders that don't necessarily follow the guidelines set by FANNIE MAE or FREDDIE MAC the agencies that set the regulations and guidelines for the mortgage industry. These lenders don't follow the rules and guidelines because the rules and guidelines are set for the entire country, meaning that all FHA's have to follow the guidelines set. They have to conform to government standards and no company in the country can do it differently than what is set for conforming mortgages.

Now, non-conforming, that's a whole other ball game.

They don't have to comply with conforming rules and regulations.

How can they make their own rules? Why don't they need to follow the government guidelines set?

The answer is simple.

They know the golden rule. If you don't know what the golden rule is, I'll tell you.

The golden rule, "He who has the gold, makes the rules". Believe it or not, and as harsh as that may sound, its absolutely true. I couldn't believe it when I first heard that and I had just come into this new industry.
I first heard it when I was questioning an underwriter as to why we couldn't or wouldn't do something for one of my clients. That's exactly what they told me! I was shocked and couldn't believe they had just said that to me. I wanted to help my client and how dare they tell me that.

I was determined to get a better answer or find another lender to help my client. I did find another lender and I did help my client. I also learned about the many different types of lenders and eventually came to the realization that they were right about the golden rule. He who has the gold makes the rules.

The B & C lenders use their own money so that's why they can make their own rules. They do non conforming mortgages that do not conform to government standards and is why they can do that. Of coarse they cannot or are not supposed to take advantage of the public, but unfortunately that's not always the case.

So since these lenders don't use the governments money, or get their money from the bond market, which is where most all other lenders and brokers get their money from, they do not have to follow the same rules.

Right about now, you might be asking yourself, why these lenders would use their own money to loan to people who have bad credit or credit issues. The answer is exactly why they do it. Its because they can make their own rules and make more money doing it. These B & C loans are high risk loans with high risk people for the most part, so guess what? The rates are higher along with the closing costs.

High risk loans, high interest rates and high closing costs. They make more on interest and closing costs to justify the risk!
Keep in mind that they still have collateral. Yes they may have a higher percentage of abandoned and defaulted loans but in the long run they've made so much more money on the large majority that the risk is absolutely worth it. They still have the home they can foreclose on, and they will not loose much money if any on these programs.

That's right! All FHA's have to comply with government standards across the entire country. They can't make their own LTV's, DTI's, or credit issues. Its black and white, No exceptions!

The same applies for all conforming mortgages. Every mortgage under the sun has to conform to government regulations. That's why their also known as conforming! Non conforming are the mortgages done by the B & C (Sub-Prime) lenders.
Since most lenders get their money for these conforming loans from the same place, that's why they have to comply.

Let me give you an example.

Jack and Shirley are shopping for an FHA mortgage. They've called ABC Lenders and ABC lenders is offering them an FHA mortgage. They'll charge the regular 1% loan origination fee and the regular costs affiliated with the mortgage. Appraisal, credit, etc.

But XYZ lenders has mentioned that they'll do the FHA with the same rate and a .50% Origination fee.

On both of these examples, neither ABC or XYZ lenders have gone over the 1% loan origination limit for FHA, but since they control what they make up to a certain extent, they can charge less if they wanted to, because they'll just make less on the loan. This is healthy and fair competition and you should be searching for these types of situations.

Now all of a sudden, XYZ lenders mentions to Jack and Shirley that They'll also go up to 98% LTV and that they'll be no MIP Fee! Jack and Shirley are a little confused. They've been told by ABC Lenders that their FHA has the MIP fee in mortgage and also told that they could only qualify up to 97% LTV on the FHA? Baffling?

This is where they're would be an issue. FHA guidelines state that the maximum allowed LTV is 97% and there must be an MIP fee. The 1.50% MIP (Mortgage Insurance Premium) is what makes an FHA. You can't have an FHA without it!

In this scenario, theres no way possible that XYZ lenders can do an FHA because they must follow FHA guidelines no matter how much they'd like to do the FHA the way they said in the second example. They could never ever do that in this entire country of ours regardless of what type of lender they are. They cannot rewrite the rules and couldn't even if they wanted to.

This is what I meant when I said all lenders must comply with the conforming guidelines. Regardless of FHA, VA or conventional. All of these types fall into conforming and all conforming mortgages must comply.

I've used this example for many years and I've heard many say, well I knew that! And I wouldn't believe someone who said that. Or a lender wouldn't say that.

Well, this is one example that has happened to me on more occasions than I can remember. The first time I heard one of my clients ask me if I could do an FHA without the MIP fee. When I said no, its impossible and that's what makes it an FHA, she mentioned that this other company had promised them that.

I wasn't sure if I heard correctly so I asked, they said they'd do an FHA without the MIP fee? Yep, she replied!

Well I saw I had a lot of explaining to do. I explained and educated her about it. She didn't believe me, so I had her call at least 5 other companies out of the yellow pages and I explained to her what to ask, specifically!

She was shocked and confused when the others told her that what makes an FHA. She asked me why would someone else tell her differently. I said, simple put, it's the famous switch and bait technique. It could also be for many other reasons. Maybe the person didn't specialize in FHA and made an honest mistake, not likely, but it could be. Maybe the person is just new and has no idea? It could be a number of things, but most likely its someone trying to mislead you into something you don't understand 100% and then obviously mislead you all the way to the closing table.

Needless to say, I earned her business and she never questioned me again. Not all mortgage professionals will look out for your best interest, so its very good that you're educating yourself so you won't have to worry about it.

Okay, so since we're talking about non-conforming mortgages, the B & C mortgages.

Using the same example, Jack and Shirley just realized that they need a mortgage with a 99% LTV. We already know that they can't do an FHA since it only allows up to 97% LTV. Jack and Shirley also cannot qualify with any company with a regular conforming conventional mortgage since the maximum allowed LTV is 95%. So what will they do?

They need to refinance. They are over extended and need to consolidate their bills and their new LTV is at 99%? This is a perfect example as to why someone would use or do a non-conforming mortgage. So now, XYZ explains that they could go to 99% LTV, but the closing costs and interest rate is higher than normal because it's a higher risk mortgage.

Jack and Shirley mention how the ABC lenders mentioned that they couldn't do an FHA to 99% LTV, or a conventional to 95%LTV. How can you guys to it. Its simple, XYZ lenders say. This is a non conforming mortgage and its not an FHA or regular conforming mortgage. That's how! We use our own money and are a sub-prime lender and we specialize in these special situations when you would normally not qualify for those other mortgages.

Ahh, does it make sense now?

Is it getting a little clearer?

They can do it, because they use their own money and it's a non conforming loan. That's the only reason they can do it. Any other way and they couldn't.

So the bottom line is know which mortgages and lenders are non conforming and conforming.

Quick overview.

The A lenders typically do FHA, VA, Conventional conforming. They must comply with government regulations.

The B & C lenders do not conform to government guidelines and do non conforming mortgages.

If it doesn't make sense, read it over a couple more times when you get a chance. It will, especially once you've done your research and have begun looking at your particular situation.

Chapter IV.

Brokers

A good Broker can be worth their weight in gold!

A good Broker will have the know how and connections to be able to get you the best possible program for you. Brokers will typically be able to offer a wide array of programs. They will typically be able to use several different lenders offering all types of mortgages to suit anyones needs. They will also be able to negotiate the best possible rates and closing costs. They will typically be able to control these two things more so than a lender.

What is a broker?

A Broker is someone who is contracted with one to several lenders and have the ability to get you a mortgage. The main difference between a broker and a lender is a lender uses their own money to loan while a broker uses the lenders money to loan. Their the middle man between the lender and you.
A good Broker will be able to do several different types of mortgages and have the know how and connections to know the proper mortgage to place you in.

As lenders there are good and bad Brokers. The same rules apply. Some specialize in A paper loans and others in the B & C loans. Some do it all!

You will have to do your due diligence finding the right broker. You'll want to use a broker who has the capabilities to do any mortgage under the sun. This will give you the most protection by allowing the broker to be able to place you in the right situation and allowing the broker to collect commissions on any program.

In other words, the broker would have no reason to place you into the wrong program because they'll get paid either way, so why put you in the wrong program and risk loosing you to the competition should someone give you information to that fact.

Once again, its not that all brokers or lenders are bad. The main reason most would put you into the program that might not fit your needs the best would simple be because they don't have the right program for you. It wouldn't necessarily be a lie if they told you that is the best program you would qualify for. For them that is.

So be prepared and know the lingo. If you read this book, you'll have all of the information and lingo to make a well informed decision and not be taken advantage of.

80% of all mortgages done is done through brokers and is one of the reasons why in a lot of cases a broker can get better rates and closing costs. The lenders know that and is why they give better rates to brokers, or at least the good brokers.

What makes a broker?

A broker in many states is required to study the mortgage industry and test in order to prove that they have enough knowledge to practice home finance. There is a brokers license required at times. These licensing issues are not what I consider a real mortgage broker to be.

In my opinion and the opinion of many, a mortgage broker is someone who is the middle man sort to speak who makes the deals happen. A broker technically is someone who uses someone else's money to loan you. That to me is a broker.

I've been a mortgage broker for many years, and a good mortgage broker is worth their weight in gold! That is no joke. I've been able to place people in mortgages that even seasoned veterans had no clue even existed. The seasoned veterans I'm speaking of in many cases are well known and have been in the business for 20 plus years.

These seasoned mortgage veterans are well educated in many cases, but most just do a hand full of mortgage programs, and once they've achieved the level of success they are looking for, that's it. Finito, they have no interest in continuing to educate themselves. Therefore they never continue searching for better programs and really never adjust to the changing economy, industry or new and better ways to help their clients or even future clients.

Those aren't the type of mortgage professionals you would want to work with. Just like doctors, lawyers, CPA's, and financial planners have to continue there education so do good mortgage brokers. Most industries develop new and better ways of doing things, and that is the same case in the mortgage industry. So when searching for the right mortgage broker, make sure it is one that has the most knowledge possible, not just with one type of mortgage, but with all of them. Do not just take there word for it, test them out.

When to use a broker?

Me being a broker and all, I would say you should use a broker when ever you can. But you must be careful. Would I always recommend a broker? No absolutely not! Why wouldn't I? It is very simple! Just like banks and lenders, not all brokers do all type of mortgages. So in reality, I would rarely if ever recommend to use a bank, lender or broker that doesn't do every type of mortgage under the sun. If they cannot do everything, then in my opinion, it would be very hard to look out for your best interest. How could you or why would you trust a banker, lender or broker if they didn't do every mortgage under the sun?

This is what I've been telling my friends, family and clients over the years. A good rule of thumb is to only work with brokers that can do any type of mortgage under the sun. I believe it is the only way to get the best of all worlds. What do I mean by that? Well, I mean, you would get the right mortgage for you. Out of all mortgages out there, you will be able to get the one that is right for you. You would also be working with someone that has the ability to negotiate the closing costs and the interest rate. Notice how I didn't say either or, but both. Brokers have that ability. Most bankers and lenders do not have the ability to do both. When they do have the ability, they have a lot of red tape to go through in order to get what you want. It is a scary way to do it, because you are at the mercy of the market and might loose out on a great rate and or program.

With major bankers and lenders it is also harder to negotiate, because most of the mortgage professionals you will be working with have higher salaries than brokers. They are looking out for their employer instead of you and their employer knows it, so what they're employer does is give them incentives and bonuses for the more money they profit per transaction (You). So the more they profit the business, then the more they'll also earn.

Notice how I said they have higher salaries than brokers, but they rarely earn more than brokers. Brokers are commission driven and usually have little to no salary, but they tend to look out more for your best interest, since they're almost always trying to beat the nationally known bankers and lenders so they beat them and earn your business by giving you something better. Typically in the form of a better rate, mortgage and closing costs. They are also going to try and do this quickly, since they need to eat. The banker and or lender will typically course you because they have the time to wait you out. They don't care as much as the broker, because of their cushy salaries which guarantee they'll eat and their employers know it.

SO in the long run you the customer suffers and they more often than not get what they want.

Types of brokers

Like bankers and lenders there are many types of brokers. There are brokers that deal primarily with good credit people.

There are brokers that deal with only bad credit people. There are brokers that deal with both. But this isn't all brokers, those are the types that deal with the types of consumers.

There are also brokers that deal with good credit and conforming mortgages. There are brokers that deal with good credit and non conforming mortgages. There are brokers that deal with bad credit non conforming mortgages, etc, etc.

See, this is when and how things start getting confusing, because I can also throw in the brokers that deal with good and bad credit non conforming, and such.
So never the less, I'm sure this isn't what you're planning on doing for your career, so I'm not going to go into such detail to explain each of these types of mortgage broker.

All you should really know is that if you choose to work with a broker, you should work with one that does ever type of mortgage under the sun. A broker that also works with every type of credit under the sun, it goes hand in hand, but you just need to make sure. This is one of the best ways to protect yourself and get the best possible deal.

The good, bad and ugly brokers

I think we covered this in detail in the previous section. I just want to remind you that there are good, bad and very ugly brokers. But this does not just apply to brokers, it applies to all lenders, bankers and brokers.
Just like any industry, there always going to be these types of companies and more importantly individuals. You can select a good company, but if you deal with the wrong person, you will have the same problem.

Just be aware of this and educate yourself so you can protect yourself. Don't expect someone else to do it for you!

Chapter V.

Credit

What is Credit?

Credit, credit can be viewed in many different ways. But the bottom line is credit is a grading system that lending institutions will look at to make a decision if you are a good credit risk or bad credit risk. This means that they will decide based on your past pay payment history. This payment history will be on signature loans, car loans, revolving credit, etc.

Credit is one of the most important things that will affect your life. Most things you will encounter will have such an impact as your credit will in your life.

If you wanted to buy a car, your credit will either help you get an automobile or hurt the chances you will have getting an automobile loan. If you wanted to get an apartment, your credit will also either help you get it or not get it. A phone for the apartment, electricity, furniture, etc.

Okay so you have all of that. Okay, so how about another angle. What if you met the girl of your dreams and fell in love. You would like to buy this gal a wonderful engagement ring, but if you do not have good credit, this will affect your ability to buy this wonderful gal an engagement ring. This can go both ways you know. I believe that a woman can also get engaged if they'd like. I'm old fashioned, but I think this can go both ways, so I'm not saying it has to be the guy, the gal could also want to buy an engagement ring and ask him to marry her? The point is, if you do not have the cash to buy the ring, you better at least have a good credit standing so the jewelry store will extend you the credit you would like.

You're probable thinking, well I already have all of that. Well, credit is also the deciding factor on business loans. If you wanted to start a company, you will use your credit to either help start your company or not. If you wanted to purchase an already established company, the same thing applies. Unless the owner is just going to allow you to make payments to him or her, you will need credit.

As you can see, credit is one of the most important things that will affect your adult life, so be very careful with your credit. One of the most important things I can tell you is maintain your good credit history! Pay attention to your debts and credit obligations. Bad credit will negatively affect your life in many ways.

If you have bad credit, you better start figuring ot a way to begin repairing your credit status. This is essential! I'll also teach you how to start reparining your credit with the bonus credit repair chapter.

If you are like most Americans, owning your own home is a major part of the American dream. There are steps you can take to get closer to your dream of homeownership. One step is to establish good credit, especially if you have had credit problems in the past. Establishing good credit might mean taking care of your debts or getting in the habit of paying your bills on time. Or it might mean creating a nontraditional credit history if you have never borrowed before. Another step is to keep your good credit once you have it. These steps can take time and determination, but they can be done. This guide will show you how.

The guide explains what credit is and why having good credit is so important, especially when you want to buy a home. The guide also provides useful information about:

- Credit reports and credit scoring
- Improving your credit
- Creating a nontraditional credit history
- Using a budget, checking account, and savings account to take control of your credit

We hope the information in this guide will help you establish and maintain good credit and move you closer to your dream of homeownership.

What makes Credit

Credit is made by the creditors that report your paying habits to them. These creditors report your account to the credit reporting agencies. The creditors will report when you established your account, what the payments are and your balance. For instance, they will report your balance of the loan on your automobile. If it is a credit card they will report the balance or amount of your available credit. As time passes, they will also report the balance as going down from your payments. They will also report the monthly payment amount.

Creditors will also report if your payments are on time or if they are late. If they are late, they will report how late they are and how many times. So if you are more than 30 days late, they will report 1 time more than 30 days late. If you have been late on 2 occassions and both times more than 30 days late, they will report 2/30's which means you were more than 30 days late paying your bill on 2 separate occasions. They will also report of you were more than 60 days late and how many times and also more than 90 days late and also haw many times.

Creditors will also report when it was. Were you late recently, this year, last year etc. This all has an affect on how a creditor views you and also will have a dramatic affect on your credit score.

When to use credit?

This is simple. I guess you should consider using credit when you do not have the cash to make a purchase for something you either want or need. Also if you do not want to use your cash reserves for a purchase. You should also use credit to establish credit. If you never establish or have credit you will need to establish credit to get credit. Make sense?

Credit should be used whenever it makes sense, but mainly credit is used for larger purchases that have a higher cost than average. Typically someone would use credit when they don't have the money for a purchase and they want the item now. It may take some time to save up the amount needed for furniture. If you wanted furniture for your new home, you may need or want $3,000-$5,000 worth of new furniture. You may have used your cash reserves for the down payment on your new home? Or you may not want to use the $3,000-$5,000 that took you so long to save, so you may want to use credit and make installment payments and pay for the $3,000-$5,000 of new furniture over time. In that situation it may also be worth it to you to pay additional interest payments which will be charged for the credit. What ever the reason, you should use credit when it makes sense, but when ever you use credit, you should use it wisely. All too often I have seen many of my clients use credit unwisely and in the long run it has cost them. In many cases you could over extend yourself to the point that you may not be able to maintain your credit installment payments which will then cause you to have late payments which will obviously hurt your credit. In this situation this will hurt your chances of qualifying for the important things.

I have also seen situations that my clients have overextended themselves to the point that they can no longer qualify for a refinance which would save them a lot of money. It would make sense to refinance and the mortgage company would love to refinance them because it would help them make their payments which would also benefit the mortgage company since the mortgage payment would also be made on time. But unfortunately one of the qualifying things is the debt to income ratios (DTI), so in these situations that you may over extend yourself, even though you may not have ever even been late on your payments, you may not qualify for many things including refinancing your home or automobiles because of your new debt to income ratios.

The bottom line is this! USE CREDIT WISELY!!!

Credit is one of the most important things in your adult life, whether you are wealthy, un wealthy, intelligent, or not, educated or not, a home owner, business owner and everything in between!!

The good, bad and ugly credit!

Unfortunately, there is so much to cover that it is difficult to identify each one of these issues. I have seen some of my clients that have had a bankruptcy 3-4 years ago that have very good high credit scores in the 700's. I have also seen people that have never been lat eon any of their payments have lower credit scores in the low to mid 600's.

Why is that you ask? I really could not answer that. As far as I am concerned the credit reporting agencies decide what credit scores people should have by throwing a dart on a credit score dart board? That is how much of a mystery credit scores are.

It is almost like the Kernels KFC recipe.

But a rule of thumb is pretty much common sense.

Good credit is credit that has no;

- No Late Payments
- No Bankruptcies
- No Charge-Offs
- No Judgments
- No Maxed Out Credit Cards
- Not a Lot of Open Accounts
- Not Too Much Credit
- Will Not have their credit cards maxed out

Bad Credit will Typically Have;

- Will Have Late Payments
- Will Have Bankruptcies
- Will Have Judgments
- Will Have Too Much Credit
- Will Have All Credit Cards Maxed Out
- Will Have Reposessions
- Will Have Charge-Offs

The Ugly Credit Will Typically Have;

- All things that are negative to credit.
- Late Payments
- Bankruptcies
- Judgments
- Foreclosures

- Charge-offs
- Repossessions
- Late Payments After Bankruptcies
- Overextended Credit
- Too Much Credit
- Credit Card Accounts that are higher than the balance
- Etc, etc.

You should really look at the categories listed above and see which area you fit into the most. You should really try to establish and maintain good credit. You should also be aware that bad credit will follow you around just like a bankruptcy. Late payments will stay on your credit up to 7 years. Even something as simple as a bounced check can and will most likely stay on your credit for up to 7 years. So be very careful and do not let simple credit mistakes affect and hurt your quality of life. Or the quality of life of your family, future love and or future children.

How to use credit for a better loan?

A consumer can use their good credit standing to re-qualify for a new mortgage (Refinancing), car loan, lower credit card rates, etc, etc.
There are many reasons someone did not get the best possible loan, mortgage when they first got their mortgage or loan. Typically it is not only because of their credit. Maybe a consumer did not have enough money to put down? Maybe the consumer did not have much established credit? Maybe the consumer had no established credit. There are many reasons why a consumer may not have gotten the best mortgage or loan when they first did it. One thing is for sure! Regardless of the reason, that mortgage or loan is a temporary situation that can and should be remedied as soon as the time is available and the one main qualifying topic will be the consumers credit.
Using credit to get a better loan means using a good standing not over extended credit to get the best and lowest possible interest rate and closing costs. It is very important and will either help your quality of life or hurt it. Remember that.

Credit Scores

Credit scores range from 400 to 900. 400 being the worse which would make 900 the best. Although you'd have to be late on every single item you've ever had credit with and file bankruptcies and have repossessions, and such to have a 400 credit score. I have literally reviewed tens of thousands of credit reports and have only seen a handful credit scores in the 400's. It's not an easy thing to do.

On the same note, I've only seen a handful of credit reports that are in the 800's. That too is not an easy thing to do. You could have never been late on anything in your entire life and have credit for 30 years and still not be worthy enough for an 800 credit score.

The credit scoring is done through the credit bureaus. They control it, no one else.

How your credit report reads

Your credit report will report public records such as;
Bankruptcies
Judgments
Collections
Late payments
Most public records are negative. Why would there be a positive public record. The items, bankruptcies, judgments, collections, late payments are what makes bad credit and will hurt your credit score.

Negative credit even if for only $50.00 could stay on your credit for up to 7 years, maybe even longer. So it is imperative that you take care of the small accounts. Swallow your pride and pay them. Even if you are in the right, pay the accounts. You are only hurting yourself when you refuse to pay these minor accounts. Well, you also hurt your family and any future relationships that you might have. You also take an added risk of not being able to take advantages of opportunities that may present themselves to you.

Bad credit is no joke, so take it very serious and don't let your pride get in the way.

What will also hurt your credit scores even if your not late on payments is the balance of your credit card accounts versus the credit limits. If you're accounts are maxed out your scores will drop. If you go above your credit limits, your score will also drop dramatically. So be very careful not to go over your limit or max out your accounts, and if you do max your accounts out, make sure to make a big effort to try and pay them down.

Chapter VI.

Bonus

Credit Repair

Credit Repair has become very controversial and confusing over the past few years. Credit has become so important in the lives of so many consumers of all walks of life including families and business people along with business owners that I've decided to throw in a bonus section on credit repair.

Many consumers and businesses believe that credit repair doesn't exist. We'll that's not 100% accurate. While it's true that you may or may not have much luck removing items that are 100% accurate on your credit report. It's also true that you may or may not remove items that do report on your credit report when actually correct.

Inaccurate, incorrect, outdated and misleading information may be removed from your credit report.

Not only that, but even items that you may have already paid for may continue to have an adverse affect on your credit report. So you should now only know your rights as a consumer when it comes to your credit, but also know what to do when something is not reporting properly or if there are some items on your credit report that as a consumer you may be able to remove.

Don't be fooled by companies charging a lot of money to help remove items on your credit or companies that charge high amounts of money to consolidate and negotiate your debt. Each of those companies apply the same exact techniques you will be learning from this chapter. This chapter will help you understand your credit and how it reports and what bankers and lenders look at.

Oliver P. Maldonado

A brief summary of your rights under the Fair Credit Reporting Act (FCRA)

The Fair Credit Reporting Act (FCRA) was designed to maintain and promote accurate, fair and privacy of information in the credit files of all credit reporting agencies. Most credit reporting agencies are agencies that gather and sell information about you. This information about you contain things such as if you pay your bills on time or if you have filed for bankruptcy. This information is provided to almost anyone who properly requests the information about you which include creditors, landlords, employers and other businesses. You can find additional and the complete information on the FCRA, 15 U.S.C. SS1681-1681u, at the federal trade commission's website (WWW.FTC. GOV). If you do not have access to a computer or the internet, then you could look in your phone book and or call information and get the number for the federal trade commission and I believe you can request a copy directly from the ftc.

The FCRA gives you the specific rights outlined below. You may have additional rights under state law.

A Brief Summary of Your Rights Under The Fair Credit Reporting Act

♦ You must be told if information on your credit report was used against you.
   Anyone who uses information from a credit reporting agency to deny you of credit, insurance, employment, or uses the information against you for any other reason must tell you. They must also provide you with the name, address and phone number of the credit-reporting agency that provided the information.

♦ You can request a free copy of your credit report.
   You can request a free copy of your credit report. You are entitled to onew free credit report per year, unless you have been denied credit or there has been action taken against you from information that came from information on your credit report if it is within 60 days of the denial or

action/*.3. You may also request a free copy if there are other special circumstances such as unemployed and looking for employment, on welfare, or there is inaccurate information due to fraud. In other cases the credit reporting agency may charge you up to $8.00.

♦ You may dispute inaccurate information with the credit reporting agency.
Every consumer can dispute information reported in their credit file. The consumer reporting agency must investigate the item(s) within 30 days. The credit reporting agency must provide information you provide to the creditor, unless your dispute is considered frivolous. The credit reporting agency must provide to you in writing the results of the investigation, and a copy of your report if the investigation results in any change. The credit reporting agency must also provide the changed information to all other credit reporting agencies.

♦ Inaccurate or unverifiable information must be corrected or deleted.
Any information that has been disputed that cannot be verified whether correct or not must be deleted from your credit report if they cannot verify within 30 days. If there is a change in your credit report resulting from your dispute, the credit reporting agencies cannot reinsert into your credit report the disputed item unless the information source verifies its accuracy. The credit reporting agency must also notify you in writing telling you it has reinserted the item. They must also notify you of the name, address, and phone number of the information source.

♦ Inacurate information must be corrected or deleted. A Credit Reporting Agency must remove or correct inaccurate or unverified information from its files, usually within 30 days after you dispute it. However, the credit reporting agency is not required to remove accurate information unless it is outdated or cannot be verified. If there is a change in your credit file resulting from your dispute the credit reporting agency cannot reinsert into your credit file unless the information source verifies its accuracy and completeness. The credit reporting agency must also include the name, address and phone number of the information source.

♦ You can dispute inaccurate information with the source of the information. If you communicate with anyone such as a creditor who reports to a credit reporting agency that you dispute an item, they may not report the information to a credit reporting agency without including a notice of your dispute. Also, once you have notified the source of the error in writing, it may not continue to report the information if it is in fact an error.

What your credit report discloses

Credit reports will most likely vary slightly depending on the agencies in their appearance. Regardless of the appearance, most credit reports will iclude.

Your Identification information: Your full name, last two addresses or more, social security number, date of birth, place of employment maybe even previous employers (If they have received that information). The term of emplyment along with income are typically not reported. Beware of the employment because if it is reported incorrect, you may have an application rejected because of it if they cannot verify employment. In addition if you are self employed, some creditors may report it as unemployed which should be corrected immediately.

Detailed information on accounts that are listed: Name and issuer, date account was opened, original balance or limit, current balance (Beginning with the reporting date, which also listed), terms of account, and the current status of the account. The status of each item is indicated by the complicated code system that identifies exactly what has occurred and has happened with the account. There is no reoom for guessing.

Public record information: A lot of public records will be included in your credit report. Bankruptcies, tax liens, judgments and other such filings.

Credit report inquiries: Each and every time someone like a bank, creditor, employer, apartment leasing company, requests or pull a copy of your credit report it is reported on your credit report as an "Inquiry" by the credit reporting agency or credit bureau. This can be looked as a negative by other credit agencies. If you have inquiries with no new open accounts that can be seen as a negative because the person looking at it will assume that you were turned down for credit. There could be other explanations, but never the less, it could be looked at as a negative. The credit bureaus have also adapted this assumption and have begun subtracting points from your fico score. Each inquiry can lower your credit score by 5-8 points.

Consumer Statement: It is your right to include in your credit report a free 100 word consumer statement. This would allow you to place a response to something in your credit report that you would like anyone looking at to understand a little more about what has happened, or explain something that might not appear fair in your credit report.

You have the right to view your credit report: There was a law in the late 90's that was placed in order to allow consumers to be able to view their credit report from any creditor. So in other words if you are speaking with a car finance department, or banker, lender, etc. If they have a copy of your credit report, you can ask to see it and they must allow you to review your credit report. In the past, they were not required to show you if you requested. Now they must. You should look at your report every time a creditor has one in front of you. There could be additional information you were not aware of. Or there could be an additional mistake and such.
They are not required to provide you with a copy. That does not mean you cannot ask for one though. I provide copies when asked from

my clients when they ask me. I believe that is an extra added value I provide to them. Why not? They can look at it, but I cannot give a copy? I would disagree with that. So go ahead and ask for it! Keep in mind, you should ask before you have made the final financial decision, they may not want to provide you with a copy if you are not purchasing their product. One reason so you do not go to their competition and get a better situation since you are empowered with your credit report.

Another reason is plain and simple out of spite. If you are not moving forward and purchase their product, why would they do you a favor? I disagree with this, but there are a lot of creditors will and do.

How to get a copy of your credit report

It's very easy to get a copy of your credit report. There are many different ways to go about it. I would recommend to stay away from the online free credit reports being offered now. The reasons behind my statement are very simple. One reason is because some of the so called free reports, it is sometimes required for you to enter your credit card information. Well that makes no sense. Why? Very simple, because they want to give you a free credit report and then they want you to sign up for this other product that they will bill you for if you don't cancel first. So what typically happens is you will sign up to receive this free credit report and then forget to cancel within the 30 day period and then you are stuck with this other service you have no use for.

Another reason is because they want to market you. But they are intelligent companies and would like to market people online that have a credit card to purchase online, so the online surfers with no credit card accounts are sorted out.

Another reason, is because the company offering you the free credit report will market services to you for services they have that meet your credit level. How would they know what your credit is like? Simple, you gave them permission to look at it when you ordered your free report. SO what services are these? Cell phones, insurance, auto loans, credit cards, etc, etc.

Last but not least, some of these so called free online credit reports are coming from companies that sell your information. Yep, you heard that correct. It is from online list companies that mek their money selling your information to other third party companies. This is called targeting the right prospect. They are selling the information about you to companies that are targeting people with your type of credit. Whether good or bad, they are going to resell your information to companies that need people with bad credit. Oh, no matter what your credit is, you have been approved for, such and such. Or your good credit standing has allowed us to lower your, such and such.

These are the companies that you have to watch out for the most, because you are going to be marketed by and your information is going to be sold to several dozen if not hundreds of third party companies. Junk mail, emails, and such.

So how can you get a free copy of your credit report.

There are a few ways I would recommend. Each consumer has the right to receive one free credit report per year from the credit bureaus. That is right, if you request on in writing and mail it to them, they will send you one free credit report per year. That is a start.

Keep in mind that with these other so called online free credit reports, it could show on your credit as an inquiry. This is negative as I mentioned before, it could lower your credit scores. There is another way which will not mentioned in the following paragraphs.

Each consumer is also allowed to receive a free copy of their credit report each time they are turned down for credit or employment. In other words if you apply for credit and are sent a letter stating you were turned down for credit or employment, you can make a copy of that letter and send it to the credit bureau and they will send you a free copy of your report for you to review. It is your right.

There are additional benefits when getting your report direct from the credit bureaus. Other than the free factor these types of requests going directly to the credit bureaus, they will not lower your credit score.

You can use one of the templates provided to order your free credit report. All you would need to do is retype exactly as written, fill in the blanks where it applies and mail out to the credit reporting agencies.

The places you will send are one of these credit bureaus. Keep in mind not to send to all three, because if you send to one at a time, you could then get 3 free credit reports per year. Also, each one of these credit bureaus will report and have some minor differences reporting about you. But generally speaking for the most part, it will be similar, so you will have a good idea of what the others report about you.

Please note that when ordering credit reports through most third party companies, your credit score will most likely not be reported on there. The credit scores will typically be provided to banks, lenders, etc. They are usually not provided or not given to companies that intend to give the reports to the consumer. The reason for this is simple, they just do not want you to know what your score is. The credit bureaus believe or assume that this is a benefit for the creditors, not the consumers. The consumer should know what is on their credit report but not necessarily a benefit to the consumer, when in actuality it is very important for the consumer to know.

TRW
P.O. Box 2104
Allen, Tx. 75002
(800_ 682-7654

Equifax
P.O. Box 105873
Atlanta, Ga. 30348
(800) 685-1111

Trans Union Corporation
P.O. Box 390
Springfield, Pa. 19064
(513) 771-3090

Here is a 10-Step Strategy to Repair Your Credit

Step 1

• Get a copy of your credit report, preferable a free copy. Use one of the templates provided in this chapter to write a letter to request a free copy of your credit report from one of the three credit bureaus.

So, although this may seem very simple as the first step, this is the step that most people get stuck at. Believe it or not, this is a fact. Most people tend to have one trait very similar to each other and that is the horrible trait of procrastination. If you have gotten this far, then you may not fall in to that category. Most also have the belief that they will learn something for them to repair their credit that will automatically repair their credit.

Do not be fooled! There is no credit repair system on earth that I know of that there is no effort in order to repair. There is however a system where you would not have to put an effort in. That is credit maintenance, which simple put is knowing what not to do to damage your credit and then you would only not do that?

If you would like to repair your credit, do not procrastinate and take action and put in an effort, The rewards are there, so just follow through.

Step 2

- With your credit report in hand, you must now take some time to carefully identify your credit problems.
I strongly recommend making at least two copies of your credit report. I recommend this because you may want to mark up the credit report in order to keep a better track of the errors. You would not want to mark up the only copy you have.
You should also make some notes on separate sheets of paper. Make a comment about each individual account that you have questions on, and or specific comments regarding those accounts you question.
Each credit report will also tell you exactly where and what to look for. They will tell you what is hurting or helping your credit. That is where you should start.
- What credit problems are you looking for? You want to find the negative remarks or better remark the "Dings" in your credit report and circle them on one of your extra copies. The negative information on your credit report are typically marked or coded similar to a bank statement, but not quite. The Fair Credit Reporting Act (FCRA) requires credit bureaus to explain anything on your credit report that you cannot or may not understand. Most if not all credit reports depending on where you get it, will contain a key to symbols to familiarize yourself with the symbols. Make sure you study and understand these symbols.

- The track record of the credit accounts being reported in your credit report track, report and record your monthly payments.

Hopefully, it is not reporting "past due" symbols which may reflect late payments which are viewed as 30's-60's-90's-120's. So if your report shows 1-30 that would mean that you have had 1-30 day late payment on that account. If it reports, 3-30's and 1 60. That would mean you where late on that account 3 times when you where 30 days late and 1 time where you where 60 days late.

In my opinion, I would say almost 90% percent of the bad marks or dings on your credit report will be those of late payments, the 30's-60's-90's-120's. Some of those marks can be incorrect or entered accidentally. The mail could have been late, they could have held your payment for a few days before posting to your account, delays in processing, etc. Then again, you could have just made the late payments, and that does not make you a bad person. Keep in mind that you have your payments posted to your accounts before the due date, not just sent or mailed to them by that time, in order to avoid those late symbols.

- There is a comments section that contain remarks such as "charge-off or charged to p & L". This is a credit account reported on your report that was never paid by you. Those accounts are very bad. It would be the equivalent of a repossession or foreclosure. Yes, that is right. Accounts that report that are not good, remember that.

What these accounts represent are accounts that you never paid for and it means that the creditor had to charge off the account or charge off to profit & loss. What does that mean? Well that means that since the account was never satisfied they charged the account to profit and loss in order to get a credit or not be taxed in their taxes. So being charged off means that they gave credit and the credit was never satisfied. Like repossession, that is why it looks very bad.

Let me give you an example how a creditor looks at this.

Imagine if your mother lent your brother or friend some money a few weeks ago. Your mother lent them $1,000 and then this same person your mother lent the money too comes up to ask you to lend them $1,000. Well, you would like to help them out, but you are an intelligent person, so you tell them in a day or too. You wanted to call your mother (Creditor) and ask her if and when she lent them money. Your mother (Creditor) says she lent them $1,000 about 3 months ago (Information on your credit report) and that they have not made one payment on time yet (3-30's) and that she might just forget about it and take the loss (Charge-off).

So you being a wise person tells them you do not have the money available to loan (Loan Denial). This is exactly how creditors view this and they make decisions based on information reporting about you on your credit report.

• Inquiries reporting and made by other creditors will appear on your credit report. Remember these in most cases will typically lower your credit score 5-8 points. Too many inquiries will look very negative for a couple of reasons. As mentioned before other creditors looking at that will wonder if you received any new accounts not reporting yet on your credit report. They will also wonder if any of them did not grant you credit and if not. Why not? What does the other creditors know that they do not, so sometimes too many inquiries can look negative.

Another reason is as we've already covered, because it may and will lower your credit scores.

The next question is, how many is too many? Well this is going to depend on the different types of creditors and there policies. Typically 4-5 inquiries in a 2-3 month period is considered too many. Rule of thumb, do not allow anyone to pull your credit is you are not 100% sure you want and are going to buy what you are looking for. If you are sure you are going to buy a car or anything on credit for that matter. You should do your research first and make sure to shop for the item over that same weekend in a 2-3 day period. Most credit bureaus are taking into consideration that you may be shoping at several places and not only one, so if they see 3-4 car stores have pulled your credit they will consider this one inquiry and will not ding your credit score each time. This is the rule of thumb, I've seen the credit bureaus make mistakes in this area.

- Public records may and can also appear on your credit report. These public records are ones such as tax liens, bankruptcies, court judgments and such. These also need to be verified with a fine tooth comb to also verify its accuracy.

Step 3

- Prepare letters of protest (Examples Included) to send to the credit bureaus disputing each "ding". This is exercising your legal rights and in order to exercise your rights to the fullest, you must aggressively challenge any and all bad marks or "dings". The credit bureau will only investigate the facts if you assert that they are in error. So don't be timid. Stand up for yourself and your rights! Prepare an aggressive but polite protest for each item you would like to challenge and tell them you are exercising your rights under the Fair Credit Repair Act (FCRA), 15 USC section 1681i.

- Let me give you an example: Let's say that you found the code "charge off" on your credit report. This code as explained earlier means that the creditor charged your account off to profit and loss and that the creditor thinks your debt is uncollectible. You could protest that this code or comment should be removed because, in fact the debt is and has been satisfied, therefore should not be reported as a charge off. You might have even paid the creditor but the creditor forgot to note this in your credit report.

- Another issue might be the past due accounts that are reporting on your credit report. You could dispute that those payments were delayed due to a mix-up with the post office when you changed your address. More often than not the the credit bureaus and the creditor will state that the payment was in fact late, and therefore it is correctly reported. However, if the mix-up really did occurr, you could submit a consumer statement to the effect that the account in question is in dispute because statements were not delivered to the creditor even though you had provided a change of address to the credit bureau.

Step 4

- Send the prepared dispute letters using the sample template letters that is provided at the end of this chapter. Select the appropriate letter and retype or hand write and fill in the blanks with your information added. You should n ever send a form or pre-printed letter as they will think it has been prepared for you and therefore not valid.

- When sending out the dispute letters, you must send them to all three credit bureaus. You want to also send each letter certified return receipt requested. This means that the letter is going to be certified that the credit bureau received it. The return receipt requested is for the post office to send to you a return receipt, so you can prove that you sent it to them. Remember, that they have 30 days from receiving your dispute to prove or delete. So this is for your protection and is what you'll use to get the credit bureaus to delete.

Step 5

- Contact the credit bureaus and creditors by telephone. If the credit bureaus and creditors are not cooperative, do not give up. Be persistent and continue disputing the account. Before you begin calling, study the information you are disputing. Gather all of the information and make sure you are well aware of the information reported which you are disputing. Before the calls write down all of the points you want to go over with the creditors. Be prepared and make sure to cover all of your points.

Step 6

- Be persistent! You must be persistent, sometimes the first letters and calls do not work or have no affect. Do not be discouraged, this is a process and you must remember that. The credit bureaus aren't in the business of deleting information. They are in the business of keeping it on as to have leverage over you. Do not be shameful or bashful or discouraged. Although it may seen hopeless it is not. Remember that. It will in most cases take some time. There have been many, many situations that result in the disputed items to be removed, but more often than not it will take some time. So be persistent and stick with it.

- Once you have talked the creditor or credit bureau to change the status of the credit account. Get the name and number of the person you are speaking with, along with their direct line and extension. Ask which location they are working at. Also let him or her know that you would like to send them a letter stating the agreement you have both come up with and if he or she could sign and send back. You should also ask if they have a standard letter that they will send to you.

- These letters are very important in case the creditor forgets to delete this information from your credit report you could verify it and send yourself to the credit reporting agencies or the credit bureau. This is also a letter you could send with the information of the person who you have made the agreement with.

- Make sure that when you get this letter and after 30 plus days have passed that you check your report again. Mark the negative marks that have been deleted or corrected.

Step 7

- Try and try again! Remember be relentless! Wait a few months and continue the process again. After some time has lapsed the situation may have changed. Once time has indeed lapsed try the creditor and credit bureaus again. Let's see what happens. When I say repeat the process, I mean the entire process. Send the certified receipt requested letters, make the calls, etc, etc. After a few months, the last few people that reviewed your requests may no longer be there. Someone with a different point of view may be looking at your next request? Or the creditors policies may have changed? Or any number of things could happen, so just start the process over again.

- So remember, you may end up dealing with a new person who would like helping you reestablish and regain a good credit standing.

Step 8

- Okay, after this process and know you have received correspondence stating that there have been some changes to your credit report compare the old reports to the new one. If you do not have a new report, make sure to get a new one. Follow the process as stated before to order a new report. Most credit bureaus will send you a new report when ever they have removed, deleted, or corrected items on your report. Make sure to note the improvements on your report. You can highlight the negative items that have moved up to a non rated or negative information that is no longer reporting as negative. It is highly unlikely that you will receive positive results from each of your disputes. So you shouldn't expect to receive 100% of the disputed items changed. But you should see some. The more you continue to follow up, the better.

- Remember that the bureau may delete some negative items for the simple reason that the creditor failed to respond in a timely fashion. It is very common for creditors to fail to respond to an annoying piece of paper. This is when the tide turns and this is now in your advantage, which will help you clear these negative "dings" on your credit report.

Step 9

- Negotiation! When all else fails, you should try to negotiate with the creditors. After you've done this process several times over a few months. Which ever items are still reporting negative on your credit report, you should try and negotiate with the creditors.

- Every creditor appearing on your credit report will have an address and phone number you could send a negotiation letter to and also follow up with a call.

- There is a negotiation letter already prepared with the other templates, you just have to fill in the blanks. Now when negotiating, we're not looking at negotiating for the full amount and the penalties and interest. We're looking at paying anywhere between 40-60% of the balance owed, without the interest and penalties. Also, this negotiation is not to just pay the account to a zero balance. This negotiation is about taking care of the debt at a discounted rate and at the same time having the creditor sign a letter that you will prepare stating the terms of the negotiation. Also removing the negative information about the account along with reestablishing the account. This is a great way to get items removed and or at least not reporting negative information on your credit report.

Step 10

- Repeat the process again. Continue over and over until your credit is repaired. Keep in mind that there is no such thing as credit repair, other than this. This is it folks. There is no other way to repair your credit. You have probable heard or read about credit repair or credit repairing agencies. Don't believe it. As much as I wished it was true, it is not. If it were, I'd be more than happy to write another book on that. I could benefit from it as well as help a lot of people if it was true.

- So continue to repeat the process over and over again until you get your credit in good standing. When you've tried and tried again, consider section 9. That is the only other way to get items removed or cleared from your report.

Following are some example letters that you should retype as it appears and fill in the blank information with your information.

You will also want to send the letters to all three credit reporting agencies and you will send the letters "return receipt requested". That way you can prove when the letters where sent out and the credit reporting agencies will now that as well.

Without the return receipt requested you will have no proof of the day the credit reporting agency received your disputes and demands.

Sample letter 1 Request to delete accounts

Date

Re: Request to Delete Accounts

Dear _____:

This letter is to confirm our telephone conversation on (Date) regarding the settlement of the above account.

As discussed, I will pay your company the amount of $_____ as full settlement of this account. Additional terms include _____.

Upon receipt of this above consideration, your company has agreed to change the entry on my credit file to "paid satisfactory." In addition, any adverse credit information regarding my account, such as "late payment" or "charge off" should be deleted from my report.

If you agree to the aforementioned terms and conditions, please acknowledge with your signature and return a copy to me.

Upon receipt of this signed acknowledgement, I will immediately forward you a cashiers check in the amount stated above.

_____   _____

Signature of Authorized Officer Date

Sample letter 2 Request of Supplemental Credit History Information

Date

Re: Request of supplemental Credit History Information

Dear Sir/Madam:

Please include in my credit report the supplemental information attached.

According to the Fair Credit Reporting Act (FCRA), 15 USC section 1681b, "It is the purpose of this title (FCRA) to require that consumer reporting agencies adopt reasonable procedures for meeting the needs of commerce for consumer credit, personnel, insurance, and other information in a manner which is fair and equitable to the consumer, with regard to the confidentiality, accuracy, relevancy, and proper utilization of such information in accordance with the requirements of this title. "The intent of the FCRA includes recording supplementary credit information if requested by a consumer.

Accordingly, I request that you add the attached history of payments, under the FCRA, 15 USC section 1681i.

Thank you for your attention. Please inform me within the statutory 30-day time period from your receipt of this letter of your compliance with the 15 USC section requirements that all information in a consumer's credit report be reflected with "maximum possible accuracy."

Sincerely,

Sample letter 3 Complaint Letter to Delete Inaccurate Information

Date

Dear Sir/Madam:

I received a copy of my credit report to find the following item to be in error. See the attached copy of the credit report. Below, I have explained the discrepancies in the numbered entries:

_____

_____

By the provisions of 15 USC section 1681i of the Fair Credit Reporting Act of 1970, I demand that these items be reinvestigated and deleted from my record. Send me names and addresses of individuals you contacted so I may follow up.

Since 30 days from receipt of this letter is your allotted time under the law to reverify these entries, it should be understood that failure to do so within that 30-day period constitutes reason to promptly delete the information from my file (FCRA 15 USC sl1681 (5) (A).

Also, pursuant to 15 USC section 1681 (6) (A) of the Fair Credit Reporting Act, please notify me when the items have been deleted. You may send an updated copy of my credit report to the below address. According to the provisions of 15 USC section 1681j, there should be no charge for this notification.

Sincerely,

Sample letter 4 Request For Credit Report

Date

Re: Request for Credit Report

Dear Sir/Madam:

Please send me a copy of my credit report.

Enclosed is $_____, as payment for the credit report.

Sincerely,

Sample letter 5 Request for Free Credit Report

Date

Re: Request for Free Credit Report

Dear Sir/Madam:

According to the attached letter, which says that my credit application was denied, your credit bureau issued the report which was used for my credit evaluation.

The Fair Credit Reporting Act of 1970, 15 USC section 1681g provides the credit bureau should send me information which led to denying my credit application. According to the provisions of 15 USC section 1681j, there should be no charge for this information.

Please send me my credit report to the below address. Additional information identifying my account is on the attached letter that denies me credit.

Sincerely,

Sample letter 6 Request to Update Account

Date

Re: Request to Update Account

Dear Sir/Madam

Please note that under Section 1681c of the Fair Credit Reporting Act you are obligated to delete obsolete information from my consumer credit report. Please refer to the information circled on the attached copy of my consumer credit report. It is obsolete and should be deleted immediately from your credit files.

Also, pursuant to section 1681i (d) of the same act, I am entitled to notification that the items have been deleted. Please send an updated copy of my credit report to the below address, as well as to any other party that has inquired about my credit rating in the last sic months.

I anticipate your immediate attention to this matter.

Sincerely,

Oliver P. Maldonado

Sample letter 7 Final Follow-up on Failure to Respond

Date

Dear Sir/Madam

On _____, I sent you a follow-up letter pointing out that you had failed to respond to my disputes of certain items found on my credit report, issued by your company. Copies of that letter and the original dispute letter are attached.

To date you still have not fulfilled the intent of the Fair Credit Reporting Act, which requires your bureau, as a consumer reporting agency, to maintain and unsure that "is fair and equitable to the consumer."

Also, the law (15 USC s1681e) stipulates that credit bureaus will "Follow reasonable procedures to assure maximum possible accuracy of the information concerning the individual about whom the report relates."

These requirements have not been met by your actions, you have not given me evidence that you have acted in a prompt or "fair and equitable" manner.

1) You have not submitted evidence of investigation by giving me names and addresses of persons contacted, nor have you removed anything found inaccurate.
2) You have not removed any item for which no verification could be made.

Since you have not met your obligations under the FCRA 15 USC 1681j, to delete any inaccurate or unverifiable information in my file within the 30-day allotted time I demand that these accounts be deleted.

Sincerely,

Sample letter 8 Request to Merge Inquiry with Account

Date

Re: Request to Merge Inquiry with Account

Dear Sir/Madam

I recently received my credit report and located problems of inaccurate reporting . A copy of the credit report is attached, with the item numbers marked.

The presence of the inquiries as entries separate from the resulting accounts inaccurately duplicates information. The inquiries reflect an incomplete and inaccurate processing of information in my file. The inquiry entries should be removed, or at least merged into the accounts to which they belong.

Under the provisions of the Fair Credit Reporting Act 15 USC section 1681i, please reinvestigate and delete these disputed items. Send me names and addresses of the persons contacted. Thirty days from receipt of this letter is the length of time you are allowed under 15 USC section 1681 (5) (A) to complete these actions unless you notify me otherwise. It should be understood that failure to re-verify within this time constitutes non-verification, and the items must be promptly deleted according to Section 1681i (A).

Also, pursuant to 15 USC section 1681i (D) of the Fair Credit Reporting Act, please notify me when the items have been deleted. Send an updated copy of my credit report to the below address. According to 15 USC section 1681j, there is no charge for notification of changes on my credit report.

Sincrely,

Sample letter 9 Demand for Corrected Credit Report

Date

Re: Demand for Corrected Credit Report

Deear Sir/Madam

On _____, I wrote to tell you I had not heard about specific actions taken to re-verify the items I had identified as inaccurate or incomplete in my credit report. Copies of my correspondence are attached for your review.

Since you have not given me names of persons you contacted for reverification of the information nor have you complied with the statutory time period of 30-days to request for reverification, I assume that you have been unable to reverify the information I have disputed. Therefore, you must comply with the provisions of the Fair Credit Reporting Act, and drop the disputed items from my credit report.

I demand that you send me a copy of my updated credit report showing the elimination of the items which I disputed on the attached letters. This copy must be provided free, according to the USC section 1681j. I demand that it be postmarked within 5 days after signing the certified mail receipt for the letter you are holding.

If I do not receive an updated copy of my credit report with the disputed items dropped, my attorney will pursue my legal rights under 15 USC section 1681n or 1681o of the Fair Credit Reporting Act, "Civil Liability for willful noncompliance."

Sincerely,

Sample letter 10 Consumer Statement

Date

Re: Consumer Statement

Dear Sir/Madam

According to the Fair Credit Reporting Act 15 USC section 1611i (B), I have the right to enter a "consumer statement" in my credit report. I have disputed the accuracy and completeness of the items circled in pen on the attached credit report.

Since reinvestigation has not resolved my dispute, I want the following statement, without alteration, included in my credit report to set forth the nature of my dispute for others to see:

_____ _____ _____ _____
_____ _____ _____ _____

According to the Fair Credit Reporting Act, please send me a free updated copy of my credit report with the above statement included.

I assume that 15 days from receipt of this request represents a reasonable time for completing the update, unless you immediately notify me otherwise.

Sincerely,

Sample letter 11 Explanation for Delinquent Payment

Date

Re: Explanation for Delinquent Payment

Dear Sir/Madam

It has recently come to my attention that several of my payments to your account have been labeled "late" on my credit report.

I have been prompt in paying in the past, and missed the payment due to _____ _____.

Since the late payments occurred for the above excusable reason, please correct the payment history for my account at the following credit bureaus, which carry your account histories:

_____
_____

It is important that my credit report reflect the good relations I have had with your company in the past. The corrections in the credit report will make it more representative of my financial habits.

Appreciate your assistance.

Sincerely,

Sample letter 12 Reminder to Respond

Date

Re: Reminder to Respond

Dear Sir/Madam

Thirty days ago you received my letter disputing several items listed in my credit report, issued by your firm. The items were inaccurate and incomplete. I have attached the original letter.

Under the Fair Credit Reporting Act 15 USC (5) (A), you have 30 days from receipt of this letter to respond to my request for reverification of the erroneous items. Since you did not immediately write to inform me of the need for additional time, presume you accepted the 30-day time limit.

I have not received a reply from you within these 30 days. Therefore, it must be that the information on my report was either inaccurate, or it could not be reverified. In either case according to the provisions of 15 USC section 1681i (A), the items must be deleted immediately.

Please respond immediately so that I do not need to pursue my legal rights under 15 USC section 1681n or 1681o, which require your compliance with the law.

Also, pursuant to 15 USC section 1681i (D) of the Fair Credit Reporting Act, please send me notification that the items have been deleted. Send an updated copy of my credit report to the below address, as well as to any other party that has inquired about my credit rating last 6 months. According to the provisions of the 15 USC section 1681j, there should be no charge for notification of changes to my credit report.

Sincerely,

Chapter VII.

Closing Costs

What are Closing Costs?

Closing costs are obviously one of the most important things regarding a mortgage whether it be with a new home purchase, refinance or any number of other mortgages.

There is added confusion with closing costs because some costs with some types of mortgages aren't allowed, while others are. If that was not enough, there are third party costs affiliated with every mortgage that adds to the complication?

First of all, lets identify closing costs. This is going to sound a little complicated and I will be including an example along with what is known as the Good Faith Estimate (GFE), that every mortgage has which has almost all of the closing costs broken down.

Closing costs have a bad nick name which is "Junk Fees". I hate this term, especially since it does not cover or explain anything that deals with closing costs. In my opinion it does the exact opposite. By the name itself, "Junk Fees", it sounds as if those fees do not belong, or that they may be negotiable. Or even that you may be taken advantage of with those fees included.

Don not get me wrong, indeed some of those fees may not belong. Some of those fees may be negotiable, but by stereo typing all of the fees with such an ignorant word, is ridiculous.

Let me explain another way, If I asked you to identify the so called "Junk Fees", which ones would you tell me they are? Which ones are needed? Are you starting to get the picture?

Let me try and break it down a little further. Is an appraisal a fee that belongs or not? It Absolutely belongs, with out it, you couldn't qualify for a mortgage since you would not know what the loan to value (LTV) is, therefore now knowing what program to be placed in. How about the credit report, does it belong or not? Of course it belongs and is a necessary. Without it, the lender would not know what type of program to place you into. How about the title fees, recording fees, attorney fees, etc, etc.

So, if you can not identify which fees belong or not, how can one give them such an idiotic name? I personally believe that the name was implemented by a mortgage professional of some kind that was comparing his or her closing costs with one of their competitors. That is my opinion, and I am pretty sure I am correct, but who knows?

Now, do not let that fool you, although there are definitely fees associated with each mortgage, these fees can also be negotiated. It is not that the fees will just disappear. The fees are not going away, it is only the fact that some times the lender or broker will be paying for them. Once again, with most mortgages there are a lot of fees that are absolutely necessary, and if the lender says they don't have appraisal fees, it is not that they don't have it. It only means that they will pay for it and if they are going to pay for it, they do not have to disclose on the good faith estimate.

Now, all fees are negotiable. But I just said that there are some fees that are absolutely necessary. That is true, but I also said that the lender might also pay for some of those fees out of their own pocket, if they are willing to. Also be aware that with some mortgage programs, there are fees that the lender is not allowed to pay by law.

We will not be covering every fee associated with each mortgage type, there are just too many programs and different policies that a lot of lenders follow. There are many different types of closing costs for each program and different combinations that will also get very complicated.
Let us not forget about why you purchased this book. You purchased it because you wanted to educate yourself and learn more about mortgages. This does not mean that you want to become a mortgage professional, so it also means you are doing this to save money, lower your interest rate, save money on interest payments and of course lower your closing costs. You will be able to do this with out having

to know every single cost that is affiliated with each mortgage. You will just need to know how to negotiate and what to say to your lender in order to get them to pay for some of those costs, whether they are affiliated with the mortgage or not. Whether they are necessary or not, so do not worry that we are not going to dissect this topic.

What are third party costs (Hard Costs)?

That is a good question that most mortgage holders do not understand and most mortgage professionals do not cover with their clients, why I do not understand.

Third party costs are costs affiliated with the mortgage that is paid to a third party company.

For instance a credit report, that is ordered through a third party company. Most mortgage lenders and brokers can order it at the comfort of their computers at their desks, but keep in mind that they are not a credit reporting agency, so although they might order the report. They are ordering it through one of the three repositories or one of there hundreds of affiliates.

The same applies to appraisals, that is a third party cost. Keep in mind that most mortgage companies and lenders are not appraisal companies, so although they might order the appraisal. The appraiser typically does not work for the mender or broker. They work for another company.

The same principle applies to many other fees, including one of the largest, which is the title. Yes, there is a third party company that is the title company.

Third Party Costs and a lot of them are third part fees, meaning they are fees going to a third party company.

Types of closing costs

Closing costs, this is an area that is very confusing. Most consumers wouldn't begin to really understand what closing costs are, let alone each type. This is done on purpose and was set up for many, many years this way for that exact purpose. To confuse consumers. Just like the casinos in Vegas are set up so people can get lot and not be able to find there way out, this is a tactic that many mortgage companies have set up many decades ago and unfortunately it has continued over the years. Most lenders or I should say most lenders employees and loan originators wouldn't be able to give the average consumer a straight answer either. For instance, if you asked 10 loan officers working for the same lender or banker what their standard closing costs are, you would surely get 10 different answers! I'm normally not a betting man, but in this case, I'd be willing to bet almost anything that you would, but don't take my word for it, try it for yourself.

The reason is very simple when you think of it. Most lenders and loan originators, loan officers and brokers have the power to charge what ever they'd like. The banks and lenders want the loan, they don't make their money on the closing costs, so since they don't make their money on closing costs, they don't care what their associates charge. They do however care what rates are given, and the lenders, bankers and such will give the originators, officers and brokers extra money when they increase the rates on the loans. It's like a thank you for making us more money, but it's also strong encouragement for them to charge higher rates. Getting back to closing costs, that is exactly most mortgage professionals couldn't give you a straight answer. The answer is what each of them would charge individually. Some are more aggressive than others, so they'll charge more. Some shouldn't be in the business and give the farm away, just kidding, but in reality, when someone charges very, very low closing costs, it's typically because they really don't know what they're doing. It's like the old saying, "You get what you pay for". That is the truth. But as the same saying goes, when you have a mortgage expert, that can do any mortgage under the sun and has contacts, and lenders, and brokers all jumping through hoops for "Me" them, you also get what you pay for. I for instance charge what I'm worth and also what you'll get. In other words, my clients will have piece of mind. What I've said will be done, plus I have a staff of professionals that will all go above and beyond to do almost anything we need to get the job done! You won't have any horror stories here. You are not going to talk to someone a few months later and find out you are in the wrong program, or not saving as much as you could be, etc, etc.

So is it worth it to pay more for service, peace of mind and the right situation for you? Absolutely it is! Just ask the people that got taken advantage of, or the ones that put their eggs in the cheap basket to only have the basket break and loose all the eggs. I've unfortunately seen way too many times when someone went with a cheap loan officer and they were strung on for so long working on a loan that they couldn't even qualify for and then two months later, they lost the rate and now can't even qualify for the one they should have been in the first place. So in these situations, they were abused way more than anything, they're now loosing thousands of dollars, dollars that could help their financial situation! So remember, you get what you pay for, and it's worth paying for quality that will put you in the right situation that's best for you!

Now, I had to go into that much detail, because if I didn't, how could I possible explain what you should expect as far as closing costs go. I'll be giving you some typical scenarios and explaining the hard costs. Hard costs are costs that you're going to have regardless of which lender you go with. With almost all mortgages you're going to need an appraisal right? So that is a hard cost, meaning you'll have that cost with most of them and it's not their cost. The lender will also have to do a title search and make sure you really do own the property, right? So that too is a hard cost, meaning it doesn't matter which lender you use, that's going to be a cost that's there regardless and it's not the lenders fee.

So remember, a hard cost is a cost that all or almost all lenders will have, but its not their cost, but it must be charged. Make sense?

So, let me give you an example of some of the hard costs.

Example Hard Costs (Typical Costs:

- Credit Report
- Appraisal
- Title Search
- Escrows
- Recording Fees

These are typical hard costs. There are sometimes additional costs that could be the lenders or brokers hard costs. This means that a broker might actually have a processing fee, which is their hard cost but not because its typical, but because the lender they are using is charging them that fee. Just look at the example hard costs, and those are the typical ones. Any other ones are negotiable, not to mention that the examples aren't, they are also negotiable, but only for the simple fact that the lender or broker might elect to pay the fees themselves. If they are earning enough money on the loan, it might make sense for them to pay the $300 appraisal fee if they will make $2,000? Wouldn't you?

So remember, most if not all fees are negotiable, and you must negotiate your closing costs the same way you'd negotiate to buy a used car. I don't know many people that pay sticker price, or pay what ever price the salesman told them. Now it's not that bad to negotiate when you know what to say, so that's why you need to know what to say. Use the terminology, mortgage vernacular. Most brokers and lenders I know will take off fees when they think the client knows what they're talking about and that's only when they mention hard costs, or that's a lender fee, not typical, etc, etc. Not rates. Most consumers assume that if they ask for rates, the lender will think they know what they're talking about. That's just not the case with experienced mortgage professionals. It was the case 20 years ago, but not in these times. So don't ask for the rates, ask what they're hard costs are, and then when they tell you, say okay, now, before we move forward, how much of that are you willing to pay for me? Or, Let's cut that 1% origination to a half % origination fee, I know that goes to you.

See, also don't ask about points, that's a dead give away that you don't know what you are talking about. Points? I've had people even mortgage professionals ask me is there any points. I'll usually say, well didn't you look at the good faith estimate I gave you? I know that's where it's disclosed? I know sometimes it's necessary to qualify? Never the less, when someone asks me if theirs points? I know they really don't know what they're talking about, sol don't fall for it. Just ask them to get rid of that?

Also junk fees? What are those?

No closing cost mortgage

Is there really such a thing of a no closing cost mortgage?

Is this a myth? Or is it real?

The answer is no! There is no such a thing? In reality the no cost mortgage is not real and it will cost you more in the long run.

Do not be misled. There is a saying in the mortgage business, "Pay me now or pay me later but you're going to pay me"!

This is very true.

So let me show you how this works. With a no closing cost mortgage, what is happening is very simple. The lender, banker or broker is increasing the rate in order to make up for the closing costs. So yes, there is mortgages that do not have the closing costs in the front. Meaning they have the closing costs hidden in the back end.
What? Hidden closing costs, well, they're not really closing costs, but there always costs affiliated with every mortgage. SO how on earth does a lender, banker or broker make uop for those costs if they don't charge me closing costs. The answer is simple. They make it up in the back end.

You should rarely if ever do a no cost mortgage. Let us remember what I've already mentioned. The most important purchase isn't your home, it is the mortgage for your home.

That being said again, the way it works is because on the no cost mortgage, they increase the rate. You might say okay. I don't mind that or paying $60 more per month if it saves me $3,000 of closing costs. Most of the times I've heard that is because they haven't thought it out enough. So let us go over the numbers together.

Let's do the math. You would trade in $3,000 for an extra $60 per month payment. Well as you know, the average mortgage is 30 years which is 360 months. SO $60 times 12 month which is 1 year is $720 extra per year in interest payments. Now times that by 5 years, that is $3,600. So in 5 years you would have paid more than what you saved. Also keep in mind that you paid that upfront and the closing costs would have been rolled into the mortgage.
But we haven't just finished the calculations just yet. Now times that by 10 years. In 10 years you would have spent $ 7,200 of extra interest. Let us just do the entire calculation. An extra $60 dollars per month would cost you a total of $21,600 over the life of the mortgage. So you tell me. Is it worth it to do a no cost mortgage? And is it really no cost when you are actually paying $21,600 extra interest payments over the mortgage term. Is it really no cost? It cost you an extra $21,600.

So my thoughts on the non cost mortgage is don't do it! It just does not make sense. Unless you know you are going to be transferred in 1 year or less, I wouldn't do a no cost mortgage.

Now this is one of the most important documents of a mortgage transaction. The Good Faith Estimate (GFE). This is the mortgage document that contains the closing costs of the mortgage transaction. It will contain almost all costs affiliated with the mortgage. It will have the loan origination which is typical for most mortgages and is a profit for most mortgage lenders and or brokers and loan officers. For loan officers it's a little different and for some mortgage brokers, they may get a percentage of this fee, and maybe a percentage of the entire net amount.

The Good Faith Estimate will also have title fees, recording fees, escrows, etc etc. Like I said, it will contain most of the closing costs. I keep saying most of, because believe it or not there are some fees that do not need to be disclosed. These would be the Yield Spread (YSP) this is the money that lenders, banks and the such will give the mortgage professionals that is a percentage (%) based on the interest rate.

Example;

Lets say a lender will let you do a mortgage conventional mortgage with them at 6.500% fixed for 30 years. That rate is a Par rate, meaning it will not cost the mortgage professional anything and it doesn't pay the mortgage professional any additional money which is a 00% Yield Spread (YSP). Yet for the same mortgage but with a little higher interest rate lets say of 6.625% fixed, they will now give the mortgage professional a .50% yield spread. This means the mortgage professional will get an additional .50% of the loan amount or half a point. And lets say if they did the same loan with an even higher rate, lets say of 6.75% maybe now the lender would give the mortgage professional 1.00% Yield Spread which is one point.

This yield spread is a percentage which is a profit and is also known as points. Origination fees and discount fees are also known as points. Points are a percentage of the loan amount.

Let me give you an example;

If a mortgage professional is getting 1.00% Yield Spread which is also 1 point, on a $100,000 mortgage loan he would get $1,000 dollars from the yield spread or point. That is also known as back end points because it's based on the loan amount and yield spread and is not disclosed on the GFE always. Sometimes it is. If a Broker or Mortgage Professional is funding the loan in their own name they do not have to disclose the Yield Spread. But most of the time the Yield Spread will be disclosed in one of the bottom lines of the GFE and will look something like this, YSP 0-3%. Sometimes it will have the exact YSP number which would look something like this, 2.78% YSP. In that situation that means the mortgage professional will get 2.78% of the loan amount or 2.78 points which is a percentage of the loan amount and is a profit to the mortgage professional.

The Good, Bad and Ugly Closing Costs

Well, I will be showing you an example GFE and I will let you make the decision on what the good, bad or ugly closing costs are. I have mixed feelings about this. Some costs are absolutely necessary and in my opinion would be considered the good costs.

The bad costs are the costs that might also be necessary, but could also be unnecessary and could be negotiated.

The ugly closing costs are the ones that are typically known as "Junk Fees". The reason they are known as junk fees is because they are junk. It is a slang term, but one that is very applicable. By definition it is a junk fee. A fee that should not be there. A fee that has no bearing on the mortgage. A fee that is extra and no one benefits from it. Well, almost no one, the one person that will typically benefit from it is usually the lender or mortgage professional. This is just an extra way for this lender to make more money with out doing any extra work. It would be the equivalent of you the consumer having another associate punch you in at work and not working or even showing up for the shift. It would also be the equivalent of an attorney billing a client for hours not spent on working on their case. Make sense, this is why I call these types of fees UGLY!

Negotiating the Closing Costs

Almost all costs can be negotiated. Even the hard costs. Yes you read that right. Even the hard costs can be negotiated. But I am not referring to negotiating the costs and increasing the interest rate, that would be like doing the no closing cost mortgage which as I mentioned before is in my opinion a mortgage scam. It is like the saying I mentioned earlier, remember "pay me now or pay me later, but you are going to pay me".

So when I say all closing costs are negotiable, I mean they are negotiable, even the ones that are a must. Such as title, appraisal, credit report and all fees.

Now don't get me wrong, I am not for a second trying to say that you can get rid of these fees. These fees are inevitable. Some closing costs will always be there. Someone has to pay for the title search. Some one has to pay for the appraisal and title and such. Of course, no mortgage company will approve or close a mortgage with out knowing who owns the home or how much the home is worth. Please notice how I said, someone has to pay for it. This means that although the fees are and will be there, the question is who will pay for it. Part of negotiating is keeping the best mortgage for you, including the interest rate and not increasing it, then lowering the closing costs with out increasing the interest rate.

So in other words, when you get the mortgage professional to pay, cover or just simple remove these fees from the Good Faith Estimate (GFE), this simple means that the mortgage professional and the company he or she represents is just simple going to make less money on the deal. It is as simple as that, and believe me they will pay. If they don't then don't do the deal with them.

You will find someone who will. Just keep the Good Faith Estimate they gave you and put in some leg work. Fax it over to several other lenders and brokers, but as I have said before, do not allow them to pull your credit. Just get them the info they need and they should and could get you a quote. Tell them what you want. You can say I was working with XYZ company and they did not want to pay for my origination, so I will not do business with them. Or they would not lower my origination by half, so I walked and I don't have a problem walking again, so I know what I want and the question is will you give me what I want. Yes or no. I don't want either one of us to waste our time.

Trust me, if you call someone, they will give you what you want unless they just can't do it because of lack of experience or lack of resources. The reason they will and should give you what you want is because you are a freebie. The reason for this is because they did not have to work for you. They did not have to spend time or money to generate the new business (You). So they should and will most likely not have any problem doing what you would like. This is also because they do not have to sell you, you are already sold and telling them exactly what you want to move forward.

I hope this makes sense! Because I am making it pretty simple. A rule of thumb, you should never ever do business with a mortgage professional that will not lower or cover some of his or her closing costs. This is a fact, if you don't ask you don't get! These people are sales people and they are used to negotiating all day long. They are used to paying and lowering their closing costs to save the business they might loose from consumers that have decided to wait or cancel. So please they are prepared to cover some of these costs.

"A rule of thumb should be, you should never ever do business with a mortgage professional that will not lower or cover some of his or her closing costs"

Good Faith Estimate (GFE)

Here is an example of the Good Faith Estimate (GFE). Study it and become very familiar with it, it is a very important document that greatly affects your mortgage and future mortgages done.

The Good Faith Estimate (GFE) is also universal. Being universal once again means that the good faith estimate in Colorado would be the same as one in Florida. Sometimes these documents might appear a little different, but the lines and numbers will be the exact same. You should really study and become familiar with the Good Faith Estimate. This is the 2nd most important mortgage document you'll need to be familiar with.

Ask questions! If you are not sure what something is or means, do not be shy. Ask? Asking will give you the information you want to know! I'm regularly amazed at how many of my clients do not ask me questions. Even when I know they might be thinking of it, or confused about something they just don't ask. I will volunteer the information. I like to educate my clients so they can feel even more comfortable and confident that they are doing the right mortgage with the right person.
So ask questions!

GOOD FAITH ESTIMATE

Applicants:	Jack Borrower / Shirley Borrower		Application No:	Jack & Shirley
Property Addr:	123 Colorado Drive, Denver, CO 80221		Date Prepared:	
Prepared By:			Loan Program:	CONV C/O

The information provided below reflects estimates of the charges which you are likely to incur at the settlement of your loan. The fees listed are estimates-actual charges may be more or less. Your transaction may not involve a fee for every item listed. The numbers listed beside the estimates generally correspond to the numbered lines contained in the HUD-1 settlement statement which you will be receiving at settlement. The HUD-1 settlement statement will show you the actual cost for items paid at settlement.

Total Loan Amount $ **223,000**   Interest Rate **7.250** %   Term **360 / 360** mths

800	ITEMS PAYABLE IN CONNECTION WITH LOAN:			
801	Loan Origination Fee	1.000%	$ 2,230.00	PFC
802	Loan Discount	0.500%	1,115.00	PFC
803	Appraisal Fee		300.00	
804	Credit Report		65.00	
805	Lender's Inspection Fee			
806	Mortgage Broker Fee			
809	Tax Related Service Fee		72.00	PFC
810	Processing Fee		600.00	PFC
811	Underwriting Fee		250.00	PFC
812	Wire Transfer Fee			

1100	TITLE CHARGES:			
1101	Closing or Escrow Fee		$ 175.00	PFC
1105	Document Preparation Fee		165.00	PFC
1106	Notary Fees			
1107	Attorney Fees			
1108	Title Insurance		550.00	PFC
	FLOOD CERT		17.50	PFC
	CLOSING FEE TO AFC		150.00	PFC

1200	GOVERNMENT RECORDING & TRANSFER CHARGES:			
1201	Recording Fees		$ 150.00	PFC
1202	City/County Tax/Stamps			
1203	State Tax Stamps			

1300	ADDITIONAL SETTLEMENT CHARGES:			
1302	Pest Inspection		$	
	Courier Fee's		45.00	PFC

		Estimated Closing Costs	5,884.50	

900	ITEMS REQUIRED BY LENDER TO BE PAID IN ADVANCE:					
901	Interest for	3	days @ $	44.9097	per day	$ 134.73	PFC
902	Mortgage Insurance Premium					
903	Hazard Insurance Premium					
904						
905	VA Funding Fee					

1000	RESERVES DEPOSITED WITH LENDER:				
1001	Hazard Insurance Premiums	2 months @ $	per month	$	PFC
1002	Mortgage Ins. Premium Reserves	months @ $	per month		
1003	School Tax	months @ $	per month		
1004	Taxes and Assessment Reserves	2 months @ $	per month		PFC
1005	Flood Insurance Reserves	months @ $	per month		
		months @ $	per month		
		months @ $	per month		

		Estimated Prepaid Items/Reserves	134.73

TOTAL ESTIMATED SETTLEMENT CHARGES			6,019.23
COMPENSATION TO BROKER (Not Paid Out of Loan Proceeds):			
Yield Spread Premium 1%-4%			$

TOTAL ESTIMATED FUNDS NEEDED TO CLOSE:			TOTAL ESTIMATED MONTHLY PAYMENT:	
Purchase Price/Payoff (+)			Principal & Interest	1,521.25
Loan Amount (-)	223,000.00		Other Financing (P & I)	
Est Closing Costs (+)	5,884.50		Hazard Insurance	
Est Prepaid Items/Reserves (+)	134.73		Real Estate Taxes	
Amount Paid by Seller (-)			Mortgage Insurance	
			Homeowner Assn. Dues	
			Other	

Total Est. Funds to you	216,980.77		Total Monthly Payment	1,521.25

☑ This Good Faith Estimate is being provided by _____, a mortgage broker, and no lender has been obtained. These estimates are provided pursuant to the Real Estate Settlement Procedures Act of 1974, as amended (RESPA). Additional information can be found in the HUD Special Information Booklet, which is to be provided to you by your mortgage broker or lender, if your application is to purchase residential real property and the lender will take a first lien on the property. The undersigned acknowledges receipt of the booklet "Settlement Costs," and if applicable the Consumer Handbook on ARM Mortgages.

Applicant	Jack Borrower	Date	Applicant	Shirley Borrower	Date

Calyx Form gfe.frm 11:01

Truth In Lending (TIL)

Another mortgage document that is very important is the Truth In Lending (TIL). This is a very important mortgage document that most consumers and even mortgage professionals don't understand. This important document includes the famous yet confusing Annual Percentage Rate (APR). I bet if you asked 10 different mortgage professionals what the APR is you will get 10 separate answers. And each of them will b confusing.

One of the reasons the APR is so confusing is because it doesn't match the actual interest rate. What? Exactly, it doesn't match the exact interest rate but it must be disclosed by law.

Why does the APR not match the exact interest rate?

The reason for this is because of the closing costs and is why it is so important. It was because of all of the junk fees and confusing closing costs that this document was invented by the government. They too in my opinion couldn't understand the closing costs and the Good Faith Estimate was so confusing and time consuming to go through that the Truth In Lending (TIL) was invented. They put all of the closing costs in a bucket and with a very complicated equation come up with the APR and if it goes above a certain level then it could be in violation of government standards. So this document and the APR in my opinion is meant for the government and is why also in my opinion why most consumers and mortgage professionals alike are so confused by it.

But you should at least understand as a consumer why the APR is higher than the actual interest rate. The reason is simple. It is because there are costs that are financed with the loan. In a refinance most if not all costs are rolled into the loan.

As an example lets say you are refinancing a $200,000 mortgage. And you got a 6.50% fixed interest rate on the $200,000 mortgage. If there are let's say $4,000 of closing costs rolled into the loan, then technically speaking the final mortgage would be $204,000. So the closing costs are rolled into the mortgage how would you calculate that? The interest rate is based on the $200,000 mortgage loan, and not the closing costs. So the closing costs need to be recovered somehow. How will this be? Well it is recovered in the payment. So if the payment is based on a $200,000 mortgage, and if they roll the $4,000 closing costs into the payment, technically that would represent a different payment wouldn't it? Of course it would! That's where the APR comes in to affect.

So since technically the payment represents a payment that isn't the actual mortgage payment based on the rate of a 6.50% $200,000 mortgage, the government said it must be disclosed. So what the APR is disclosing is what the difference is as an example.
Confusing huh? Indeed!

So to make it simple, the APR could be looked at as the cost of doing the mortgage. I know there are a lot of unanswered questions that will remain and will always remain with this document. But the reality is, it is not your actual interest rate and is primarily intended to disclose the rolled in closing costs.

Technically speaking if there was no closing costs and no escrows rolled into the loan, no costs at all, then the interest rate and the APR would match. That is in theory! I have never done a mortgage like this and haven't seen one done this way so I can't speak from experience there.

The Truth In Lending (TIL) is also so important because it will show you this huge gigantic number$$$!! This number is the shocker of all mortgages and proves what I've always said. It's the mortgage that is the most important thing, not the hime. Look at these numbers and tell me I'm wrong.

APR

So in the far left hand corner, you will see the infamous APR.

Financed Amount
In the next box, you will see the financed amount which is going to be more than the loan amount itself.

Amount Financed
In the next box third from the left you will find the amount financed which is the loan amount.

Total of Payments Amount Financed Plus Finance Charge
In the last box to the right of all the boxes you will see the monstrous number which is the loan amount plus the financed amount and this is exactly why I've always said the mortgage is more important than your home. Pull out you Truth In Lending and I dare you to tell me I'm not right! If you don't have a Truth In Lending, look at the example I've included!

TRUTH-IN-LENDING DISCLOSURE STATEMENT
(THIS IS NEITHER A CONTRACT NOR A COMMITMENT TO LEND)

Applicants:	Jack Borrower	Prepared By:	
	Shirley Borrower		
Property Address	123 Colorado Drive		
	Denver, CO 80221		
Application No	Jack & Shirley	Date Prepared:	

ANNUAL PERCENTAGE RATE	FINANCE CHARGE	AMOUNT FINANCED	TOTAL OF PAYMENTS
The cost of your credit as a yearly rate	The dollar amount the credit will cost you	The amount of credit provided to you or on your behalf	The amount you will have paid after making all payments as scheduled
7.504 %	$ 330,308.26	$ 217,345.77	$ 547,654.03

☐ REQUIRED DEPOSIT: The annual percentage rate does not take into account your required deposit
PAYMENTS: Your payment schedule will be:

Number of Payments	Amount of Payments **	When Payments Are Due	Number of Payments	Amount of Payments **	When Payments Are Due	Number of Payments	Amount of Payments **	When Payments Are Due
		Monthly Beginning			Monthly Beginning			Monthly Beginning
359	1,521.25							
1	1,525.28							

☐ DEMAND FEATURE: This obligation has a demand feature
☐ VARIABLE RATE FEATURE: This loan contains a variable rate feature. A variable rate disclosure has been provided earlier.
CAN GO UP TO 85% LTV FOR A CASH OUT BUT NEED TO ADD .32 FOR MI
CAN GO UP TO 90% LTV FOR A CASH OUT BUT NEED TO ADD .52 FOR MI
CAN GO UP TO 95% LTV FOR A RATE AND TERM REFI BUT NEED TO ADD .62 FOR MI

CREDIT LIFE/CREDIT DISABILITY: Credit life insurance and credit disability insurance are not required to obtain credit, and will not be provided unless you sign and agree to pay the additional cost.

Type	Premium		
Credit Life		I want credit life insurance.	Signature:
Credit Disability		I want credit disability insurance.	Signature:
Credit Life and Disability		I want credit life and disability insurance.	Signature:

INSURANCE: The following insurance is required to obtain credit:
☐ Credit life insurance ☐ Credit disability ☐ Property insurance ☐ Flood insurance
You may obtain the insurance from anyone you want that is acceptable to creditor
☐ If you purchase ☐ property ☐ flood insurance from creditor you will pay $ for a one year term.
SECURITY: You are giving a security interest in
☐ The goods or property being purchased ☐ Real property you already own
FILING FEES: $
LATE CHARGE: If a payment is more than   days late, you will be charged   % of the payment
PREPAYMENT: If you pay off early, you
☐ may ☐ will not have to pay a penalty
☐ may ☐ will not be entitled to a refund of part of the finance charge
ASSUMPTION: Someone buying your property
☐ may ☐ may, subject to conditions ☐ may not assume the remainder of your loan on the original terms
See your contract documents for any additional information about nonpayment, default, any required repayment in full before the scheduled date and prepayment refunds and penalties
☐ * means an estimate ☐ all dates and numerical disclosures except the late payment disclosures are estimates

* * NOTE: The Payments shown above include reserve deposits for Mortgage Insurance (if applicable), but exclude Property Taxes and Insurance

THE UNDERSIGNED ACKNOWLEDGES RECEIVING A COMPLETED COPY OF THIS DISCLOSURE.

Jack Borrower	(Applicant)	(Date)		Shirley Borrower	(Applicant)	(Date)
	(Applicant)	(Date)			(Applicant)	(Date)
	(Lender)	(Date)				

Calyx Form - til.hp (02/95)

The good, bad and the ugly closing costs (Junk Fees)

Okay, so what are the junk fees? This is a question that is kind of confusing. I've met mortgage professionals that couldn't answer this question. I've met many professionals in industries that also deal with the mortgage industry that also couldn't answer this question.

I have a good example of this.
I was once dealing with a real estate agent that I was doing the mortgage for a client of mine that used this real estate agent for the purchase of their home. I was doing the mortgage part of the transaction. So the real estate agent asked me if there were any junk fees. I said no there's not and I also offered to fax them over a copy of the GFE, good faith estimate so they could see for themselves.
I faxed over the GFE, good faith estimate which shows the fees. The real estate agent called me back the next day and asked me the same question, are there any junk fees. I said I faxed you over the GFE, they asked what that was. I said it was the good faith estimate which has all of the fees associated with the mortgage. The real estate agent told me, oh yes I did see it, but I'm still wondering if there are any junk fees.
I started getting the impression that this real estate professional had no idea what they were talking about. This concerned me greatly because my client is also working with them and I tend to only do business with experienced professionals for the benefit of my clients. I repeated myself and told the professional no there aren't any junk fees associated with this loan. I also then explained the GFE to the agent like I would do with all of my clients. In this case, I was talking with a real estate professional, so it's seems a little tedious to say the least. I don't mind training mortgage and real estate professionals that are affiliated with my organizations or that I may have alliances with. But to explain and train a complete stranger that is not affiliated with me or any organization I do business with is not the best use of my time.

I was concerned for my clients best interest and I truly did not think my client would get the best service with this agent. It is my responsibility to notify my client of my thoughts and then to seek an alternative. At the time I was affiliated with over 20 real estate organizations that were truly experts in the field.

I advised my client and they told me they knew the real estate agent was not the most experienced and did not know much or was not even that good. They felt very comfortable with me and expected me to look out for their best interest. I said I am and is why I'm recommending we work with another real estate agent. My client then told me why we were working with this particular real estate agent. It was their sister in law and they were doing a favor for a family member.

I then still tried to explain that it is not in their best interest, but they knew I would not allow anything to happen to them. To make a long story short, I had one of the real estage professionals I worked with to do me a personal favor and look over the entire transaction and also help my client with the real estate part of the transaction. My real estate professional did me the favor, and we finalized on both deals and everyone was happy.

I left one thing out in this story. This real estate agent that was related to my client was not a rookie. This person had over 12 years of experience, not very good experience, but experience none the less. So do not be fooled by experience. Sometimes years in the business does not mean much. I guess I know why the family was trying to pitch in to help this real estate professional. Had they not, this person would have starved out of the business, which is what should happen. This person did not and does not belong in the business. No telling what damage they may do to unsuspected consumers.

This is a true story and I'm not bringing it up to scare you or impress you. I bring this to impress upon you not to trust just anyone, including family members or people with so called experience.

Be careful whos advise you take regarding junk fees. What may be a junk fee to some mortgage professionals may not be to others. What are also true junk fees may also be actual fees to some lenders and some brokers and lenders may have to have the fees in the loan, which would then make it a hard cost.

So in other words, if you are not sure what is a junk fee or not, the best thing to do is ask.

I you are not 100% sure, then just ask. If they cannot explain the exact origin of the fee and cannot explain who the fee goes to, then be very weary and ask them to remove the fee.

A typical mortgage professional will generally speaking remove the fee to save face and reestablish your trust in them. Even if the fee was supposed to be there, they would rather just make less money or cover the fee with some of the other costs affiliated with the mortgage.

Junk fees are also typically pretty low, to a few hundred dollars. Generally speaking not too much money and also in most cases not part of the hard costs I've described previously.

Chapter VIII.

Bi-Weekly Mortgages

The Equity Acceleration Program is a Bi-Weekly payment which allows homeowners to increase their Equity up to three times faster and shorten their mortgage term by nine years.

Yes, the biweekly is very affective and homeowners can indeed save $20,000-$65,000 or more on their mortgage interest. This can be done without having to refinance and everyone qualifies for this program.

The biweekly mortgage isn't even a mortgage, it's a biweekly payment plan.

You might be asking yourself right about now, is this really true? Can this really work? Well let me answer those questions for you. YES! It's 100% true and it really does work.

Here's how it works.

Lets go back to our Jack & Shirley example.
If you remember Jack & Shirley have a monthly mortgage payment of $1,521.25 with a biweekly program, every 2 weeks, half of their payment amount ($760.62) is paid. This generates an extra one-half mortgage payment for Jack & Shirley approximately once every six months which will be applied directly against their principal balance due on their loan. So, over the coarse of a year, instead of making 12 monthly payments Jack & Shirley will be making the equivalent of 13.
The two extra half payments will be used to accelerate the principal balance on Jack & Shirleys loan.

Its that simple!

Wait a minute, you're probable asking yourself if you can just do this on your own. Yes you sure can. Lets be realistic. You can make these extra payments yourself, but have you been? Will you? Most of the thousands of clients I've had over the years haven't made these types of payments. Many who have known about this program. I make sure I tell all of my clients about this and to make extra payments to principal. I actually take it a step further and offer all of my clients this service for free and I hate to admit it, but most of them do not take advantage of this. So don't lie to yourself and think you'll do it on your own.

If this is something that you think would benefit you, you should set up a biweekly program. If you're wondering how. I'd be more than happy to set one up for you. If you become a client, I'll do it for free! If not, I'll do it for a small amount!

Following will be a chart showing you Jack & Shirleys biweekly plan including their savings. Please take a moment to see exactly how much money they will save. You'll notice that in that scenario, they'll save $79,690.42 on interest payments and shorten their mortgage term by 6.3 years!! Wow!
Also notice how Jack & Shirley were able to get an effective rate of 5.73% from their original 7.25% interest rate.

You'll also notice a couple of other examples showing how much more they could save and how much lower of an effective interest rate they can get by adding just a little extra on top of the biweekly payment.

Don't get me wrong, this shouldn't be the only option you look at. You should indeed look at all options, but if you have the lowest rate possible for your situation already and or cannot qualify for a refinance, you should definitely consider this coarse of action. Well, realistically you should consider it regardless.

What is a bi-weekly?

The best kept secret in the mortgage industry!

This is one of the most effective ways and best kept secret homeowners should and need to know about.

Bi-weekly mortgages, well this is something that is very simple, but over the years mortgage lenders have complicated it in order to keep you away from it. The truth is the bi-weekly mortgage is not a mortgage at all. It is a bi-weekly payment schedule. Mortgage lenders and most mortgage professionals really dislike the bi-weekly payment schedule. It is very easy to understand why they dislike this program so much. The reason they dislike this program is because they loose huge amounts of interest payments.

Let me give you an example:

A homeowner with a $223,000 mortgage at 7.25% would save $79,600.42 in interest payments. Yes, that's right. SO as you probable figured out, that's money that would normally go to the lender, but with a bi-weekly payment schedule, in this example would save the $79,600.42

If that was not enough, in that same scenario, that same mortgage would have an effective Interest rate equivalent to 5.75%! Wow!

So let me ask you, can you see why the lenders don't like this program?

Let me go into more detail, this was all done with out having to refinance in any way. That's right! In that scenario, that was done without having to refinance at all!

Not only that, but that was also done without having to qualify. Yes, I understand that this sounds crazy, but it is absolutely true.
Everyone qualifies to set up their payments in bi-weekly installments.
It does not matter if you have had a bankruptcy, bad credit, no credit,

slow pays, etc. It does not matter, everyone qualifies for this amazing program.

This is why most lenders and brokers do not like this program. With bi-weekly payments no lender or broker could compete with that, unless they also offer the bi-weekly program.

As an example, I offer a free bi-weekly with each of my clients. I'm on their side, I want each of my clients to save as much money as possible. That's what I do. I wish I could say that for everyone.

When to use a bi-weekly

Anyone and everyone should consider doing a bi-weekly mortgage schedule. It doesn't matter if you are a new mortgage holder or have had a mortgage for many years. It does not matter if you have just refinanced, or are planning on refinancing. The bottom line is, you will save a lot of money on interest payments and receive a lower effective interest rate and everyone qualifies.

The bi-weekly mortgage payment is a great way to save tens of thousands of dollars which will give you a lower effective rate. A bi-weekly mortgage payment will also help you pay your mortgage off on average about 7-10 years early. You do the math, that adds up to many, many thousands of dollars.

If you like to save money, the bi-weekly mortgage payment is one of if not the best way to save money and get a lower affective interest rate.

Equity Accelerator

How would you like to accelerate the amount of equity your home accumulates?

How about accelerating your equity five times faster than what it would normally take?

Of course, you would be interested in accelerating your equity five times faster.

There are three ways you will get equity in your home.
One is your home goes up in value, and the mortgage balance does not go up, therefore creating more equity for you.
Two is you pay down your current mortgage balance which will increase the equity in your home, combining the amount you pay down your home mortgage along with your home going up in value will increase your mortgage at a more rapid rate.
Three is you pay your home mortgage balance down quicker than normal. At a more rapid rate, therefore increasing the equity at a faster rate.

This is where the bi-weekly really takes effect, it helps you pay down the mortgage balance at a more rapid pace, which also gives you the effective rate lower than what you currently have. You will also save thousands of dollars on interest payments, increase your equity five times faster and along with your home going up in value, you will increase your equity the fastest way possible!

Helping Your Family and Friends

Over the years, I've met and consulted with thousands of people. Homeowners, renters, realtors, mortgage professionals, financial planners, accountants, attorneys, etc. If there's one thing I've learned, it is that other than helping themselves the next most important thing from the people I've met with is helping their families and friends.

Most meet with me to help and educate themselves, but it's also as important for them to be able to help their family and friends.

Since that has been the case for the majority of my clients, I also encourage you to share the very valuable information contained in this powerful book with your family and friends. Help educate them with their mortgage financing. Help educate them in the decisions they are considering that deal with a home purchase, refinance or even a debt consolidation. Share the information contained in this book with them. Help your friends and family understand what they are looking at or hearing from their lenders or brokers.

Don't just use this information for yourself. Share your new found knowledge. You'll not only impress your family, friends and piers, but you will also help them. You will be surprised at some of the same questions you had, that they will now ask you.

Now if you are not interested in taking the time and energy to educate your family and friends, which does not mean you are a bad person or that you don't want to help them. If that is the case, then you could lend them the book after you are done. Just make sure that you ask them to return the book to you. There are some things that you'll want to review in the future if you are going to refinance your mortgage, purchase a new home or take a 2nd mortgage out.

So please do pass this information out to your family and friends, how ever you would like to. Give them the information, educate them or tell them about the mortgage book and have them go out and invest the small amount of time and funds that will definitely have a huge impact in their future finances.

Mortgage Qualifying Secrets Revealed

As I sit here in my office late at night typing away on a mission to help thousands. I think to myself. What else can I do? What else can I include in this book to try and make an impact and help people?

Well, I figured I'd go right to the source. Let me include some secrets. Please keep in mind that I'm not referring to my secrets, I'm talking about some industry secrets.

I also wanted to include some information on the process that most of my clients aren't aware of. There is a lot of things that go on in a mortgage that most aren't aware of and rarely even see. So I'm going to include some of the things that you would normally not even see when doing a mortgage. I'm going to start an application in my mortgage software and show you some other things that you may now recognize that you've learned from some of the previous chapters.

I'm going to start an actual loan for Jack & Shirley to show you how part of the process is done. I hope this helps! I'm sure this might not go well with many lenders and brokers when they see this, but I'm not doing it for them. I'm doing it for the consumers. Any good driven mortgage professional wouldn't mind this anyway. The ones it may bother will be the ones that aren't that good and I could care less for them. They make the industry look bad, but if they are reading this book, my hat goes off to them. Maybe they're trying to learn and or become better and there's definitely nothing wrong with that.

Oliver P. Maldonado

Okay, here we go.

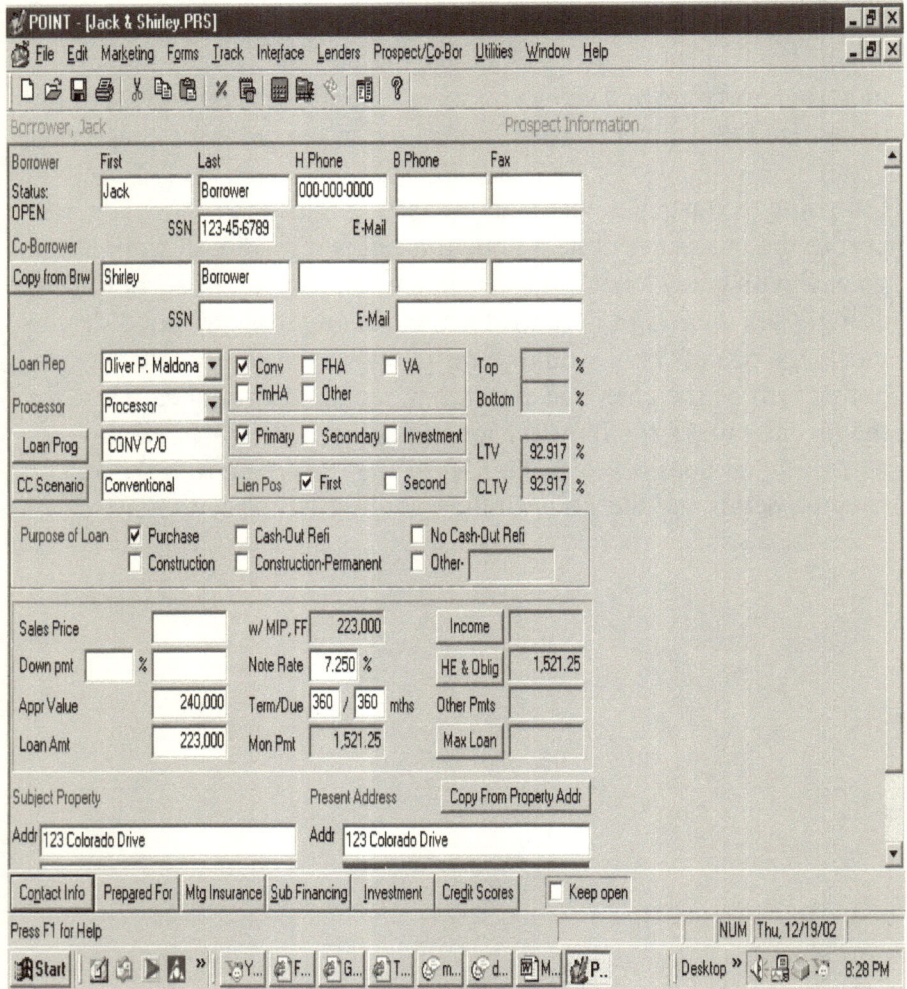

See how easy that was. I just started a new mortgage for Jack & Shirley. This is the beginning process and if you'll notice on this first main screen it has the DTI indicated with a top and bottom%. It's blank at the moment, because I have yet to input Jack & Shirleys income. Once I do that, and include their debt. I will have a DTI percentage that will help me determine what type of mortgage to place them into.

If you look at the example you'll also see an LTV and CLTV section. The LTV is for the Loan To Value the CLTV is for the Combined Loan To Value. If you're wondering, the LTV is for the 1st mortgage. But the CLTV is if there was a 2nd mortgage or if I was doing a 2nd mortgage.

You'll also see the appraised value and mortgage loan amount. The interest rate and term is also there. I also have the type of mortgage I'm looking at, which in this case shows as CONV C/O / CONVENTIONAL. Once I pull credit I'll also have the credit scores at my fingertips.

This is the screen that I use the most. With all information inputed, this is where I'll begin looking at the DTI, LTV, and Credit in order for me to be able to put Jack & Shirley into the right program. Most mortgage professionals may have a similar screen that they use.

Believe it or not, to this very day, there are many loan officers and mortgage brokers that don't have this simple resource available to them. I've seen professionals have 1003 applications and no mortgage software or system to help them place their borrowers into the right programs.

There are some other screens I have to input information also. For instance the 1003 application is where all of Jack & Shirleys information will go on.

Moving on to page 1 of the 1003 application. This section only shows a part of the application. But if you'll notice, this is where we start getting more detailed information on Jack & Shirley. I'll be including actual copies of the 1003 so don't worry that you're going to miss something, because you're not. We're going to cover everything.

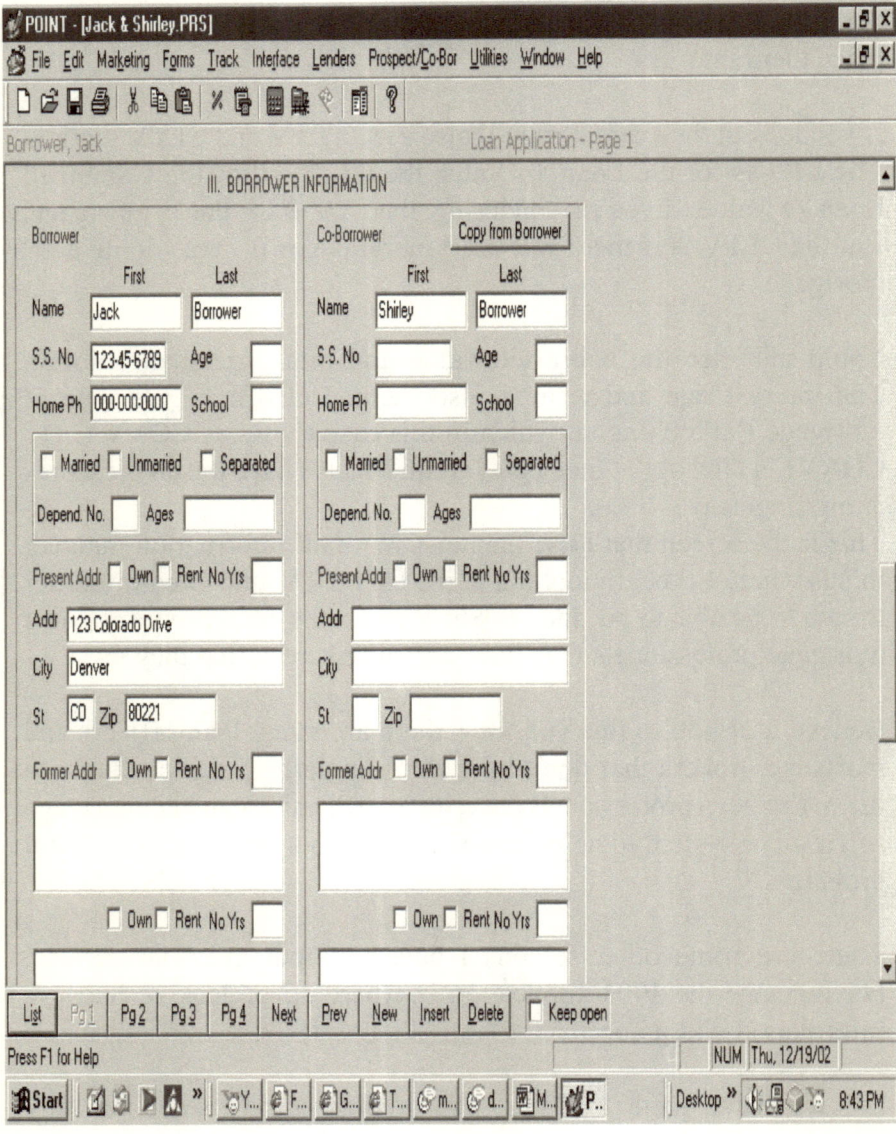

If you'll notice on this section of the 1003 application. This is page 1 and we're starting to input Jack & Shirleys information separate. They are known in the application as Borrower the first section on the left and Co-Borrower the section on the right of it.

I must tell you. I'm very exited about doing this. I've never shown the general public any of these things before. I have nothing to hide and have shown my personal clients this information, but never the general public. Well that's not 100% true. I have spoken and been featured in seminars that I've shown some of the general public some of this information, which was also exiting. I can honestly say that I have not shared this information at this level.

It exites very much to know that this will help a lot of people. Tens of thousands of people, hopefully even hundreds of thousands of homeowners. This will be the new revolution of the mortgage industry. Millions and millions of homeowners, oh, sorry. I was getting a little carried away there for a moment.
Lets get back to it! Shall we?

The next example I'm going to show you will be on page 2 of the 1003 application. Page two will have the incomes of both Jack & Shirley. Page 2 will also have the monthly mortgage payment and taxes, insurance, MI or MIP fee, to mention just a few things from the example. Page 2 of the 1003 is covered in more detail in the book. This is just an example.

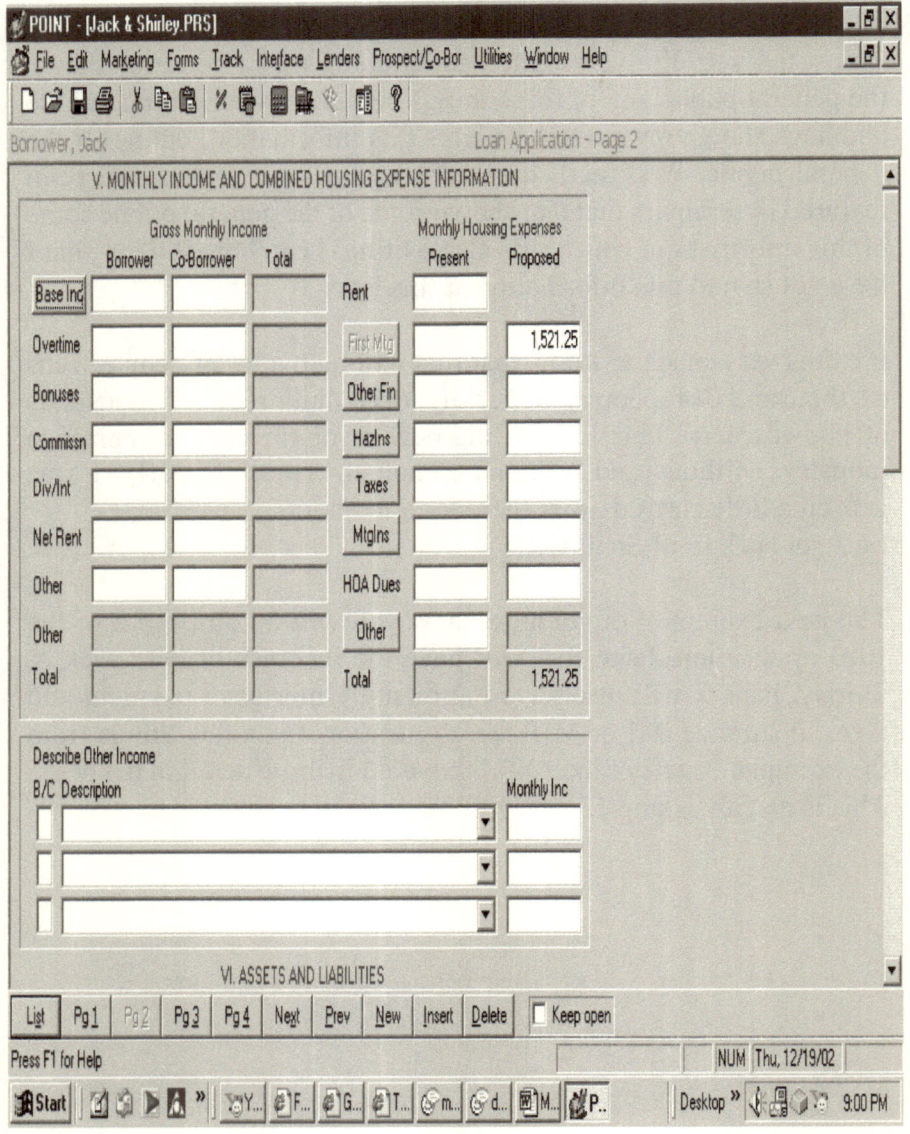

Chapter IX.

Mortgages as an investment

As we've been covering throughout the mortgage book, most homeowners look at their home as an investment and yes the home is also an investment. As we've also covered in great detail the mortgage also needs to be looked at as an investment. Its still a fact that you'll spend more on your mortgage than the home itself, and as the saying goes, a penny saved is a penny earned! Lets get back to some of the advantages of mortgages as investments. Keep in mind that this information is primarily for the average homeowner, although I love working with and helping commercial lenders and investors, the main focus of this particular book is for the average homeowner.

One of the main things I must convey before we continue is that first of all, getting the best mortgage from the beginning is the best and most affective way to make sure your mortgage is an investment. I cannot state that enough.

Some of the mortgage advantages would be the deductibility of the interest paid on your mortgage. In other words, homeowners can write off or deduct the interest paid from their interest rate on their mortgage up to 100% Loan to Value of their home.

Huh? You ask? Let me explain a little more detailed. In other words you can deduct the interest paid on your mortgage every year! That's a huge benefit! Up to 100% Loan to Value means that since some mortgages allow homeowners to borrow over or above the value of their home by going over 100% Loan to Value, they would only be allowed to deduct up to the 100% Loan to Value mark! The reason for this is obvious, the government isn't going to allow you to deduct more than the home is worth. For instance, if you have a home that's worth $100,000 and you borrowed or have a 2nd 125% loan to value mortgage or the combined loan to value on both mortgages is 125%, meaning your home is worth $100,000 but you owe $125,000, you'd only be able to deduct the interest paid up to the 100% loan to value level.

Other than getting the right mortgage from the beginning, this is one of the most beneficial benefits or advantages for homeowners.

Please consult with your tax advisor for additional information.

Other advantages for homeowners would be the fact that the home is typically appreciating in value, so you're building equity. As you make all of your payments and hopefully include extra payments to lower the principal even more, not only is your principal amount going down, but the home value is appreciating, going up!

Using the previous figures, lets say that the home you had valued at $100,000 for the past five years has been appreciating in value and over the past five years has gone up in value and now is worth $150,000. Keep in mind that you've been making all of your payments and even including extra towards the principal, and not only has your home increased in value, but you're balance now is $90,000, that means that is you subtract the balance of $90,000 and the value of $150,000 you'd have $60,000 in equity!

Now that we've gone over equity again, lets see what you can use the equity for. First of all you can let it sit. You can let it accumulate from the payments you'll continue to make along with the home which will hopefully keep appreciating in value. But if you need it its their for you to use. You can use your equity for a secured loan also known as a 2nd mortgage. You can use if for home improvements or just get cash out.

Cash out refers to either a refinance where you'd borrow more than the balance and the difference would go to you so you'd be taking cash out of your home. Cash out could also refer to a 2nd mortgage that's given to you in a check in your name, which again is taking cash out of the home.

An example would be, using the scenario again from above if you owed $90,000 and the home is worth $150,000 you could refinance and get a new mortgage paying off the current first mortgage which is the refinancing. If you refinanced with a new mortgage of $110,000 that would mean that you'd get a check or cash out of $20,000. If you subtract the new loan of $110,000 and the old mortgage balance of $90,000 the difference would be $20,000. Lets cover this in a little more detail, this example is if there were no closing costs. Since a large majority of mortgages have closing costs affiliated with the mortgage, you'd have to take that into consideration and you may actually only end up with $17,000 of cash out. That would depend on the closing costs.

Now as we discussed a moment ago, you can deduct the interest on a mortgage, so another benefit is the fact that you can use cash out from your mortgage for an auto purchase, home improvements, college fund for your kids, paying off bills, etc, etc. Some people use their credit cards, or signature loans for these items. I think its much smarter to use your equity for these types of purchases. Only if you were going to borrow it. In other words if you're still going to borrow from a bank or use your credit cards, first of all its much harder to qualify for those types of loans, not to mention the fact that the interest rates are most likely higher, these loans also offer no interest deductibility. See now you're getting it, why would someone use a high interest rate credit card or signature loan which most likely has higher rates and no deductibility benefit, when you could use the equity in your home and get the extra benefits!
Keep that in mind the next time you're taking out a loan.

Rent Vs. Own

Okay for those of you that are reading this and are renting, this is a question you've probable been asking yourself for awhile now! Right? Of coarse, so lets go over this comparison.

Renting versus owning, let me start by saying that owning is the way to go. Don't fool yourself and don't allow others to fool you either. Its always better to own than rent, and I hope to prove that to you in a moment. Some of the reasons or excuses I've heard from many of my past clients are that they're waiting for interest rates to go down. Or they're trying to save money for the down payment, or they're trying to pay off some debt, working on their credit. Just to mention a few, I know you can come up with additional reasons why you're renting or waiting to buy. Believe me, I've heard that one also and although some excuses make more sense than others, as I said before. Owning is the way to go. If you can, buy a home and don't wait.

If you're waiting for qualifying purposes, meaning you know for sure you can't qualify for a mortgage. Then that makes temporary sense, so long as you're working on resolving what ever the issue is that didn't allow you to qualify in the first place.

Don't wait until you can qualify for the home you really want. Don't wait for rates to go down, or for the raise, or anything else. The only reason you should wait and rent versus owning or buying a home is only if you cannot qualify and you're only waiting until you do qualify!

If you're renting, you're throwing money away! Its as simple as that! If you can qualify for even a starter home, and you're renting, you're throwing money away! Just know that. Even if you could qualify with a higher interest rate and high closing costs, if that's the best situation or program you can qualify for, go and buy a home. It's better to have a high rate and own than rent.

How so, you ask?

We'll when you rent, you get nothing in return for all of your monthly rent payments. Once your lease is up, you move out with nothing. All of your payments which add up to a significant amount means nothing! When the lease is up, all you do is move out. It doesn't matter that you made all of your payments on time. They're not reporting that to your credit bureau. You don't even get that benefit.

Lets say you're renting and you're paying $950 per month which sounds a little low, for the rent that's going around in the areas I know of. But lets say you're paying $950 on rent, that's $11,400 per year. Do the math, $950 times 12 months is $11,400 per year, so if you rented for 5 years that would be $11,400 times 5 equals $57,000. Wow!

So if you're renting in that example, what have you gotten for your $57,000? You've made those payments, and that's what they add up to. Notice how I didn't say this is how much you've invested over the past 5 years, because its not an investment. This is how much you've thrown away over the past 5 years. Keep in mind that when your lease is up, you move out and get nothing for that money. You don't even get any tax breaks for those payments. Nothing, no equity, no appreciation in value, nothing!

When you own a home, that $57,000 has gone to pay down your mortgage principal. That's not it, all of the interest you've paid out of that $57,000 has also benefited you with the tax benefits. So every year, you'll get a portion of that back. Every year your home has also appreciated in value.

Once again, lets use the previous figures as an example. The home that was worth $100,000 5 years ago is now worth $150,000 and the $57,000 in payments have paid down the mortgage to $90,000. So if you were making the exact same payments in this example, you would have benefited every year with the tax advantages. You would have also benefited because when you move out of the home you own and sell it, you'll pocket $60,000.

So, lets review.

Whats better? Renting versus owning?

I hope no one has said renting. If you did, read this chapter again and continue reading this chapter until you get it.

Even if you wanted to wait until rates went down, which would be the better or even smarter decision? Owning!
If instead of owning or waiting to buy the $200,000 home, which is smarter, renting and waiting for 5 years and then starting with nothing, or owning a smaller home, that in 5 years would give you the extra money you'd need to buy the $200,000 home you originally wanted? If you didn't answer with owning, read this entire section again.

If you need the down payment to qualify, of coarse, save, save and save until you have it. Be aware of the no money down programs. Also know of the owner carry homes. This means that an owner will carry the mortgage they already have in order to sell the home. It might cost a little more, but if this is the only way you can get into a home, then do it!

There are many options to get into a home, so remember do what ever you have to do in order to buy a home. Don't rent unless you have no other option, but don't be the typical person who suffers from excusitis!

Own or buy a home! Don't rent unless you have no choice and cannot qualify and if that's the case, find a broker like myself, then it'll be my job to figure it out for you. Believe me, I'll get you in a home, one way or another!

Don't worry if you'll not have the benefit of working with me. Please try and contact me, I'll be glad to help as many people as possible, but as I've pointed out, I have a large client base and although I try to get to everyone, sometimes theres just not enough hours in the day for me to be able to work with everyone. Even with a staff of people helping me out!

Don't worry though. Remember, that's why I wrote this book. In order to be able to help many thousands of people. Please use this book to learn what you need to know in order to help and protect yourself!

This book will help you! As you're read on the inside cover, I guarantee that if you read this book, you'll find the mortgage that's right for you!

Tax Benefits

Now I have to give my disclaimer here. I am not a tax advisor nor am I a CPA. I'm just giving you some ideas and you should consult with your tax advisor for further information regarding this topic and to learn what the current laws are.

Okay, so now let us move forward.

What are some of the tax benefits when it comes to mortgages? Well first of all the interest paid on your mortgage is tax deductible.

On a 2nd mortgage you can also deduct the interest paid on it up to 100% loan to value. That means that if you have a 2nd mortgage that is over 100% you could only deduct the interest up to the 100% loan to value.

Let me show you an example. If you have a mortgage for $100,000 and the value of your home is $100,000 that would be 100% loan to value. Now since there are some 2nd mortgages that go above 100% loan to value, lets say you have a 2nd mortgage in this example for $15,000 in that scenario your loan to value is 115%. So you could only deduct the interest paid up to 100%.

There are some other tax benefits also, but these are the only ones we'll be covering in this book. The purpose of this book is to help you with your current mortgage as far as savings on refinancing, purchasing, interest rates and closing costs. So this would fall into that category.

Chapter X.

Mortgage Forms

Uniform Residential Mortgage Loan Application (URLA / 1003)

One of the most important mortgage forms or documents would be the application. Also known as the 1003 (Ten 0 three), or URLA which would stand for Uniform Residential Loan Application. This is where the whole process begins and takes place.

The 1003 application is the same for all states. Some lenders rearrange part of its looks, but it is the same. The same lines and information must appear exactly for any state.

The 1003 application consists of 4 pages, the first three being important and contains all information regarding your mortgage.

Page one of the 1003 application is where you'd find the type of mortgage. Conventional, FHA, VA, etc. On the first page you'll also find the term 360/360 (30 Years due in 30 years). You'll see the interest rate, and the type of rate, fixed, 1/1 ARM, 3/1 ARM, etc.

On the first page of the 1003 you'll also see your age, education, children, most recent two years of residence, most recent two years of employment, employment address and phone numbers, etc.

All of this information will be for both you and your spouse or any person on the loan for that matter.

I'll be including a copy of the entire 1003 application so you'll know what to look for.

Oliver P. Maldonado

Uniform Residential Loan Application

This application is designed to be completed by the applicant(s) with the lender's assistance. Applicants should complete this form as "Borrower" or "Co-Borrower", as applicable. Co-Borrower information must also be provided (and the appropriate box checked) when ☐ the income or assets of a person other than the "Borrower" (including the Borrower's spouse) will be used as a basis for loan qualification or ☐ the income or assets of the Borrower's spouse will not be used as a basis for loan qualification, but his or her liabilities must be considered because the Borrower resides in a community property state, the security property is located in a community property state, or the Borrower is relying on other property located in a community property state as a basis for repayment of the loan.

I. TYPE OF MORTGAGE AND TERMS OF LOAN

Mortgage Applied for:	☐ V.A. ☑ Conventional ☐ Other: ☐ FHA ☐ FmHA	Agency Case Number	Lender Case Number

Amount	Interest Rate	No. of Months	Amortization Type:	☑ Fixed Rate ☐ GPM	☐ Other (explain): ☐ ARM (type):
$ 223,000	7.250 %	360/360			

II. PROPERTY INFORMATION AND PURPOSE OF LOAN

Subject Property Address (street, city, state, ZIP) — No. of Units
123 Colorado Drive, Denver, CO 80221
Legal Description of Subject Property (attach description if necessary) — Year Built

Purpose of Loan ☑ Purchase ☐ Construction ☐ Other (explain): ☐ Refinance ☐ Construction-Permanent
Property will be: ☑ Primary Residence ☐ Secondary Residence ☐ Investment

Complete this line if construction or construction-permanent loan.

Year Lot Acquired	Original Cost	Amount Existing Liens	(a) Present Value of Lot	(b) Cost of Improvements	Total (a+b)
	$	$	$	$	$

Complete this line if this is a refinance loan.

Year Acquired	Original Cost	Amount Existing Liens	Purpose of Refinance	Describe Improvements ☐ made ☐ to be made
	$	$		Cost $

Title will be held in what Name(s) | Manner in which Title will be held | Estate will be held in: ☑ Fee Simple ☐ Leasehold (show expiration date)

Source of Down Payment, Settlement Charges and/or Subordinate Financing (explain)

III. BORROWER INFORMATION

Borrower	Co-Borrower
Borrower's Name (include Jr. or Sr. if applicable) Jack Borrower	Co-Borrower's Name (include Jr. or Sr. if applicable) Shirley Borrower

Social Security Number 123-45-6789	Home Phone (incl. area code) 000-000-0000	Age	Yrs. School	Social Security Number	Home Phone (incl. area code)	Age	Yrs. School

☐ Married ☐ Unmarried (include single, divorced, widowed) ☐ Separated | Dependents (not listed by Co-Borrower) no. ages
☐ Married ☐ Unmarried (include single, divorced, widowed) ☐ Separated | Dependents (not listed by Borrower) no. ages

Present Address (street, city, state, ZIP) ☐ Own ☐ Rent No. Yrs.
123 Colorado Drive
Denver, CO 80221
Present Address (street, city, state, ZIP) ☐ Own ☐ Rent No. Yrs.

If residing at present address for less than two years, complete the following:

Former Address (street, city, state, ZIP) ☐ Own ☐ Rent No. Yrs. | Former Address (street, city, state, ZIP) ☐ Own ☐ Rent No. Yrs.

Former Address (street, city, state, ZIP) ☐ Own ☐ Rent No. Yrs. | Former Address (street, city, state, ZIP) ☐ Own ☐ Rent No. Yrs.

IV. EMPLOYMENT INFORMATION

Borrower	Co-Borrower
Name and Address of Employer ☐ Self Employed	Yrs. on this job / Yrs. employed in this line of work/profession	Name and Address of Employer ☐ Self Employed	Yrs. on this job / Yrs. employed in this line of work/profession
Position/Title/Type of Business	Business Phone (incl. area code)	Position/Title/Type of Business	Business Phone (incl. area code)

If employed in current position for less than two years or if currently employed in more than one position, complete the following:

Name and Address of Employer ☐ Self Employed	Dates(from-to) / Monthly Income $	Name and Address of Employer ☐ Self Employed	Dates(from-to) / Monthly Income $
Position/Title/Type of Business	Business Phone (incl. area code)	Position/Title/Type of Business	Business Phone (incl. area code)
Name and Address of Employer ☐ Self Employed	Dates(from-to) / Monthly Income $	Name and Address of Employer ☐ Self Employed	Dates(from-to) / Monthly Income $
Position/Title/Type of Business	Business Phone (incl. area code)	Position/Title/Type of Business	Business Phone (incl. area code)

Freddie Mac Form 65 10/92
CALYX Form 1003 Loanapp1.hp 2/95

Page 1 of 4 Borrower _____ Co-Borrower _____

Fannie Mae Form 1003 10/92

168

V. MONTHLY INCOME AND COMBINED HOUSING EXPENSE INFORMATION

Gross Monthly Income	Borrower	Co-Borrower	Total	Combined Monthly Housing Expense	Present	Proposed
Base Empl. Income*	$	$	$	Rent	$	$
Overtime				First Mortgage (P&I)		1,521.25
Bonuses				Other Financing (P&I)		
Commissions				Hazard Insurance		
Dividends/Interest				Real Estate Taxes		
Net Rental Income				Mortgage Insurance		
Other (before completing see the notice in "describe other income" below)				Homeowner Assn. Dues		
				Other		
Total	$	$	$	Total	$	$ 1,521.25

*Self Employed Borrower(s) may be required to provide additional documentation such as tax returns and financial statements.

Describe Other Income   Notice: Alimony, child support, or separate maintenance income need not be revealed if the Borrower(B) or Co-Borrower(C) does not choose to have it considered for repaying this loan.

B/C		Monthly Amount
		$

VI. ASSETS AND LIABILITIES

This statement and any applicable supporting schedules may be completed jointly by both married and unmarried Co-borrowers if their assets and liabilities are sufficiently joined so that the Statement can be meaningfully and fairly presented on a combined basis; otherwise separate Statements and Schedules are required. If the Co-Borrower section was completed about a spouse, this Statement and supporting schedules must be completed about that spouse also.

Completed ☑ Jointly ☐ Not Jointly

ASSETS Description	Cash or Market Value	Liabilities and Pledged Assets. List the creditor's name, address and account number for all outstanding debts, including automobile loans, revolving charge accounts, real estate loans, alimony, child support, stock pledges, etc. Use continuation sheet, if necessary. Indicate by (*) those liabilities which will be satisfied upon sale of real estate owned or upon refinancing of the subject property.	Monthly Payt. & Mos. Left to Pay	Unpaid Balance
Cash deposit toward purchase held by	$	**LIABILITIES**		
		Name and address of Company	$ Payt./Mos.	$
List checking and savings accounts below				
Name and address of Bank, S&L, or Credit Union				
		Acct. no.		
		Name and address of Company	$ Payt./Mos.	$
Acct. no.	$			
Name and address of Bank, S&L, or Credit Union				
		Acct. no.		
		Name and address of Company	$ Payt./Mos.	$
Acct. no.	$			
Name and address of Bank, S&L, or Credit Union				
		Acct. no.		
		Name and address of Company	$ Payt./Mos.	$
Acct. no.	$			
Name and address of Bank, S&L, or Credit Union				
		Acct. no.		
		Name and address of Company	$ Payt./Mos.	$
Acct. no.	$			
Stocks & Bonds (Company name/ number & description)	$			
		Acct. no.		
		Name and address of Company	$ Payt./Mos.	$
Life insurance net cash value	$			
Face amount: $				
Subtotal Liquid Assets	$			
Real estate owned (enter market value from schedule of real estate owned)	$	Acct. no.		
		Name and address of Company	$ Payt./Mos.	$
Vested interest in retirement fund	$			
Net worth of business(es) owned (attach financial statement)	$			
Automobiles owned (make and year)	$			
		Acct. no.		
		Alimony/Child Support/Separate Maintenance Payments Owed to:	$	
Other Assets (itemize)	$	Job Related Expense (child care, union dues, etc.)	$	
		Total Monthly Payments	$	
Total Assets a.	$	Net Worth (a-b)	$	Total Liabilities b.	$

Freddie Mac Form 65   10/92
CALYX Form 1003 Loanapp2.hp 2/95

Page 2 of 4   Borrower _____   Co-Borrower _____

Fannie Mae Form 1003   10/92

Oliver P. Maldonado

VI. ASSETS AND LIABILITIES (cont.)

Schedule of Real Estate Owned (if additional properties are owned, use continuation sheet)

Property Address (enter S if sold, PS if pending sale or R if rental being held for income)	Type of Property	Present Market Value	Amount of Mortgages & Liens	Gross Rental Income	Mortgage Payments	Insurance, Maintenance, Taxes & Misc	Net Rental Income
		$	$	$	$	$	$
Totals	$	$	$	$	$	$

List any additional names under which credit has previously been received and indicate appropriate creditor name(s) and account number(s):

Alternate Name	Creditor Name	Account Number

VII. DETAILS OF TRANSACTION		VIII. DECLARATIONS				
a. Purchase price	$	If you answer "yes" to any questions a through i, please use continuation sheet for explanation.	Borrower Yes	No	Co-Borrower Yes	No
b. Alterations, improvements, repairs		a. Are there any outstanding judgments against you?	☐	☐	☐	☐
c. Land (if acquired separately)		b. Have you been declared bankrupt within the past 7 years?	☐	☐	☐	☐
d. Refinance (incl. debts to be paid off)		c. Have you had property foreclosed upon or given title or deed in lieu thereof in the last 7 years?	☐	☐	☐	☐
e. Estimated prepaid items	134.73	d. Are you a party to a lawsuit?	☐	☐	☐	☐
f. Estimated closing costs	4,769.50	e. Have you directly or indirectly been obligated on any loan which resulted in foreclosure, transfer of title in lieu of foreclosure, or judgment? (This would include such loans as home mortgage loans, SBA loans, home improvement loans, educational loans, manufactured (mobile) home loans, any mortgage, financial obligation, bond, or loan guarantee. If "Yes," provide details, including date, name and address of Lender, FHA or VA case number, if any, and reasons for the action.)	☐	☐	☐	☐
g. PMI, MIP, Funding Fee						
h. Discount (if Borrower will pay)	1,115.00					
i. Total costs (add items a through h)	6,019.23					
j. Subordinate financing		f. Are you presently delinquent or in default on any Federal debt or any other loan, mortgage, financial obligation, bond, or loan guarantee? If "Yes," give details as described in the preceding question.	☐	☐	☐	☐
k. Borrower's closing costs paid by Seller		g. Are you obligated to pay alimony, child support, or separate maintenance?	☐	☐	☐	☐
l. Other Credits(explain)		h. Is any part of the down payment borrowed?	☐	☐	☐	☐
		i. Are you a co-maker or endorser on a note?	☐	☐	☐	☐
		j. Are you a U. S. citizen?	☐	☐	☐	☐
		k. Are you a permanent resident alien?	☐	☐	☐	☐
m. Loan amount (exclude PMI, MIP, Funding Fee financed)	223,000.00	l. Do you intend to occupy the property as your primary residence? If "Yes," complete question m below.	☐	☐	☐	☐
n. PMI, MIP, Funding Fee financed		m. Have you had an ownership interest in a property in the last three years?	☐	☐	☐	☐
o. Loan amount (add m & n)	223,000.00	(1) What type of property did you own-principal residence (PR), second home (SH), or investment property (IP)? ___				
p. Cash from/to Borrower (subtract j, k, l & o from i)	(216,980.77)	(2) How did you hold title to the home-solely by yourself (S), jointly with your spouse (SP), or jointly with another person (O)? ___				

IX. ACKNOWLEDGMENT AND AGREEMENT

The undersigned specifically acknowledge(s) and agree(s) that: (1) the loan requested by this application will be secured by a first mortgage or deed of trust on the property described herein; (2) the property will not be used for any illegal or prohibited purpose or use; (3) all statements made in this application are made for the purpose of obtaining the loan indicated herein; (4) occupation of the property will be as indicated above; (5) verification or reverification of any information contained in the application may be made at any time by the Lender, its agents, successors and assigns, either directly or through a credit reporting agency, from any source named in this application, and the original copy of this application will be retained by the Lender, even if the loan is not approved; (6) the Lender, its agents, successors and assigns will rely on the information contained in the application and I/we have a continuing obligation to amend and/or supplement the information provided in this application if any of the material facts which I/we have represented herein should change prior to closing; (7) in the event my/our payments on the loan indicated in this application become delinquent, the Lender, its agents, successors and assigns may, in addition to all their other rights and remedies, report my/our name(s) and account information to a credit reporting agency; (8) ownership of the loan may be transferred to successor or assign of the Lender without notice to me and/or the administration of the loan account may be transferred to an agent, successor or assign of the Lender with prior notice to me; (9) the Lender, its agents, successors and assigns make no representations or warranties, express or implied, to the Borrower(s) regarding the property, the condition of the property, or the value of the property.
Certification: I/We certify that the information provided in this application is true and correct as of the date set forth opposite my/our signature(s) on this application and acknowledge my/our understanding that any intentional or negligent misrepresentation(s) of the information contained in this application may result in civil liability and/or criminal penalties including, but not limited to, fine or imprisonment or both under the provisions of Title 18, United States Code, Section 1001, et seq. and liability for monetary damages to the Lender, its agents, successors and assigns, insurers and any other person who may suffer any loss due to reliance upon any misrepresentation which I/we have made on this application.

Borrower's Signature	Date	Co-Borrower's Signature	Date
X		X	

X. INFORMATION FOR GOVERNMENT MONITORING PURPOSES

The following information is requested by the Federal Government for certain types of loans related to a dwelling, in order to monitor the Lender's compliance with equal credit opportunity, fair housing and home mortgage disclosure laws. You are not required to furnish this information, but are encouraged to do so. The law provides that a Lender may neither discriminate on the basis of this information, nor on whether you choose to furnish it. However, if you choose not to furnish it, under Federal regulations this Lender is required to note race and sex on the basis of visual observation or surname. If you do not wish to furnish the above information, please check the box below. (Lender must review the above material to assure that the disclosure satisfy all requirements to which the Lender is subject under applicable state law for the particular type of loan applied for.)

BORROWER
☐ I do not wish to furnish this information

Race/National Origin: ☐ American Indian or Alaskan Native ☐ Asian or Pacific Islander ☐ Black,not of Hispanic origin ☐ Hispanic ☐ White,not of Hispanic origin ☐ Other (specify)_____

Sex: ☐ Female ☐ Male

CO-BORROWER
☐ I do not wish to furnish this information

Race/National Origin: ☐ American Indian or Alaskan Native ☐ Asian or Pacific Islander ☐ Black,not of Hispanic origin ☐ Hispanic ☐ White,not of Hispanic origin ☐ Other (specify)_____

Sex: ☐ Female ☐ Male

To be Completed by Interviewer	Interviewer's Name (print or type)		Name and Address Interviewer's Employer
This application was taken by:	Oliver P. Maldonado		
☐ face-to-face interview	Interviewer's Signature	Date	
☐ by mail			
☐ by telephone	Interviewer's Phone Number (incl. area code)		

Freddie Mac Form 65   Page 3 of 4   Fannie Mae Form 1003   10/92
CALYX Form 1003 Loan   hp 2/95

170

GOOD FAITH ESTIMATE

Applicants: Jack Borrower / Shirley Borrower	Application No: Jack & Shirley
Property Addr: 123 Colorado Drive, Denver, CO 80221	Date Prepared:
Prepared By:	Loan Program: CONV C/O

The information provided below reflects estimates of the charges which you are likely to incur at the settlement of your loan. The fees listed are estimates-actual charges may be more or less. Your transaction may not involve a fee for every item listed. The numbers listed beside the estimates generally correspond to the numbered lines contained in the HUD-1 settlement statement which you will be receiving at settlement. The HUD-1 settlement statement will show you the actual cost for items paid at settlement.

Total Loan Amount $ 223,000   Interest Rate 7.250 %   Term 360 / 360 mths

800	ITEMS PAYABLE IN CONNECTION WITH LOAN:			
801	Loan Origination Fee	1.000%	$	2,230.00	PFC
802	Loan Discount	0.500%		1,115.00	PFC
803	Appraisal Fee			300.00	
804	Credit Report			65.00	
805	Lender's Inspection Fee				
808	Mortgage Broker Fee				
809	Tax Related Service Fee			72.00	PFC
810	Processing Fee			600.00	PFC
811	Underwriting Fee			250.00	PFC
812	Wire Transfer Fee				

1100	TITLE CHARGES:		
1101	Closing or Escrow Fee	$	175.00	PFC
1105	Document Preparation Fee		165.00	PFC
1106	Notary Fees			
1107	Attorney Fees			
1108	Title Insurance		550.00	PFC
	FLOOD CERT		17.50	PFC
	CLOSING FEE TO AFC		150.00	PFC

1200	GOVERNMENT RECORDING & TRANSFER CHARGES:		
1201	Recording Fees	$	150.00	PFC
1202	City/County Tax/Stamps			
1203	State Tax/Stamps			

1300	ADDITIONAL SETTLEMENT CHARGES:		
1302	Pest Inspection	$		
	Courier Fee's		45.00	PFC

	Estimated Closing Costs	5,884.50

900	ITEMS REQUIRED BY LENDER TO BE PAID IN ADVANCE:			
901	Interest for	3 days @ $ 44.9097	per day	$ 134.73	PFC
902	Mortgage Insurance Premium				
903	Hazard Insurance Premium				
904					
905	VA Funding Fee				

1000	RESERVES DEPOSITED WITH LENDER:			
1001	Hazard Insurance Premiums	2 months @ $	per month	$	PFC
1002	Mortgage Ins. Premium Reserves	months @ $	per month		
1003	School Tax	months @ $	per month		
1004	Taxes and Assessment Reserves	2 months @ $	per month		PFC
1005	Flood Insurance Reserves	months @ $	per month		
		months @ $	per month		
		months @ $	per month		

	Estimated Prepaid Items/Reserves	134.73

TOTAL ESTIMATED SETTLEMENT CHARGES	6,019.23
COMPENSATION TO BROKER (Not Paid Out of Loan Proceeds):	
Yield Spread Premium 1%-4%	$

TOTAL ESTIMATED FUNDS NEEDED TO CLOSE:		TOTAL ESTIMATED MONTHLY PAYMENT:	
Purchase Price/Payoff (+)		Principal & Interest	1,521.25
Loan Amount (-)	223,000.00	Other Financing (P & I)	
Est. Closing Costs (+)	5,884.50	Hazard Insurance	
Est. Prepaid Items/Reserves (+)	134.73	Real Estate Taxes	
Amount Paid by Seller (-)		Mortgage Insurance	
		Homeowner Assn Dues	
		Other	
Total Est. Funds to you	216,980.77	Total Monthly Payment	1,521.25

[✓] This Good Faith Estimate is being provided by _____ a mortgage broker, and no lender has been obtained. These estimates are provided pursuant to the Real Estate Settlement Procedures Act of 1974, as amended (RESPA). Additional information can be found in the HUD Special Information Booklet, which is to be provided to you by your mortgage broker or lender, if your application is to purchase residential real property and the lender will take a first lien on the property. The undersigned acknowledges receipt of the booklet "Settlement Costs." and if applicable the Consumer Handbook on ARM Mortgages.

Applicant Jack Borrower	Date	Applicant Shirley Borrower	Date

Calyx Form gfe.frm 11:01

TRUTH-IN-LENDING DISCLOSURE STATEMENT
(THIS IS NEITHER A CONTRACT NOR A COMMITMENT TO LEND)

Applicants:	**Jack Borrower**
	Shirley Borrower
Property Address:	**123 Colorado Drive**
	Denver, CO 80221
Application No:	**Jack & Shirley**

Prepared By:

Date Prepared:

ANNUAL PERCENTAGE RATE	FINANCE CHARGE	AMOUNT FINANCED	TOTAL OF PAYMENTS
The cost of your credit as a yearly rate	The dollar amount the credit will cost you	The amount of credit provided to you or on your behalf	The amount you will have paid after making all payments as scheduled
7.504 %	$ **330,308.26**	$ **217,345.77**	$ **547,654.03**

☐ REQUIRED DEPOSIT: The annual percentage rate does not take into account your required deposit

PAYMENTS: Your payment schedule will be:

Number of Payments	Amount of Payments **	When Payments Are Due	Number of Payments	Amount of Payments **	When Payments Are Due	Number of Payments	Amount of Payments **	When Payments Are Due
		Monthly Beginning:			Monthly Beginning:			Monthly Beginning:
359	1,521.25							
1	1,525.28							

☐ DEMAND FEATURE: This obligation has a demand feature.
☐ VARIABLE RATE FEATURE: This loan contains a variable rate feature. A variable rate disclosure has been provided earlier.
CAN GO UP TO 85% LTV FOR A CASH OUT BUT NEED TO ADD .32 FOR MI
CAN GO UP TO 90% LTV FOR A CASH OUT BUT NEED TO ADD .52 FOR MI
CAN GO UP TO 95% LTV FOR A RATE AND TERM REFI BUT NEED TO ADD .62 FOR MI

CREDIT LIFE/CREDIT DISABILITY: Credit life insurance and credit disability insurance are not required to obtain credit, and will not be provided unless you sign and agree to pay the additional cost.

Type	Premium	Signature	
Credit Life		I want credit life insurance.	Signature:
Credit Disability		I want credit disability insurance.	Signature:
Credit Life and Disability		I want credit life and disability insurance.	Signature:

INSURANCE: The following insurance is required to obtain credit:
☐ Credit life insurance ☐ Credit disability ☐ Property insurance ☐ Flood insurance
You may obtain the insurance from anyone you want that is acceptable to creditor
☐ If you purchase ☐ property ☐ flood insurance from creditor you will pay $ for a one year term.
SECURITY: You are giving a security interest in:
☐ The goods or property being purchased ☐ Real property you already own.
FILING FEES: $
LATE CHARGE: If a payment is more than   days late, you will be charged   % of the payment.
PREPAYMENT: If you pay off early, you
☐ may ☐ will not have to pay a penalty.
☐ may ☐ will not be entitled to a refund of part of the finance charge.
ASSUMPTION: Someone buying your property
☐ may ☐ may, subject to conditions ☐ may not assume the remainder of your loan on the original terms.
See your contract documents for any additional information about nonpayment, default, any required repayment in full before the scheduled date and prepayment refunds and penalties
☐ * means an estimate ☐ all dates and numerical disclosures except the late payment disclosures are estimates.

* * NOTE: The Payments shown above include reserve deposits for Mortgage Insurance (if applicable), but exclude Property Taxes and Insurance.

THE UNDERSIGNED ACKNOWLEDGES RECEIVING A COMPLETED COPY OF THIS DISCLOSURE.

Jack Borrower	(Applicant) (Date)	**Shirley Borrower**

	(Applicant) (Date)	(Applicant) (Date)

(Lender) (Date)

Calyx Form - til hp (02/95)

Chapter XI.

Getting the Mortgage You Want

The most important thing you must know in order to get the exact mortgage you want is knowing which mortgage you qualify for and why! Sounds simple enough. So if it is so simple, then why is it that most people do not get the right mortgage for them?
The answer is simple, it is because they really do not know which mortgage they want. They do not understand much about mortgages in order to make an intelligent decision.

In other words, if a consumer meets with a mortgage professional and is asking for a conventional mortgage but they're Loan To Value (LTV) is at 97%, well I hate to be the one to point this out, but they do not qualify for an conventional mortgage. The sad thing about this is I have heard of this request all to often. In many occasions the consumer is stubborn and will not take the word of the mortgage professional. Or the mortgage professional did not explain it thorough enough to the consumer so the consumer will just go to the next mortgage professional. If that mortgage professional does not explain it in detail this consumer very well may end up doing the exact same thing and going yet to another mortgage professional.
This consumer will eventually just give up, develop a bad taste for mortgage professionals and at the same time may very well just give up never getting the right mortgage for them.
What this consumer did not know is that conventional mortgages do not go up to 97% Loan To Value (LTV). The type of mortgage this consumer needed was an FHA mortgage which does go up to 97% Loan To Value (LTV). Regardless of what this consumer wanted, it was irrelevant. I have seen this situation all to often. Consumers should not just count on mortgage professionals to be able to communicate this point to them. They should learn the basic mortgage principals and then know what they not only want but what they would qualify for.

This would be the equivalent of going to a auto dealership and asking the sales person for a brand spanking new Jaguar for the same price as a Cavalier. Do not get me wrong, I like Cavaliers but the quality is just not the same as a Jaguar. It's like going into a Ferrari dealership and asking for a Ferrari with a $200 monthly payment! It's just not going to happen no matter how many Ferrari dealerships you go to. And since it is such an unusual request, they will most likely not take you seriously enough to want to spend the time educating you.

I have seen all too often many mortgage professionals that would rather just not deal with this type of consumer and would instead just move on to the next consumer in line.

So the first rule in getting the mortgage you want is knowing which mortgage you qualify for, then you can make an educated decision and then select the right mortgage for you.

I have always told my clients that if they want a mortgage that they do not qualify for, it is not the right one for them. And it does not matter how many companies or mortgage professionals they go to, no mortgage company or professional could do that type of mortgage.

Negotiating

In today's mortgage industry consumers who are not prepared with the basic knowledge of the mortgage industry and those who are not motivated enough to negotiate for their mortgage will have a huge price to pay. It will inevitable be the costliest mistake they will most likely make in their life. As I've said through out this book, most consumers and professionals alike have been misled to believe that their home is the most expensive purchase they will ever make which as you have seen with my calculations which are very real, the mortgage is far more costly than the home itself. The mortgage will cost more than the home and not by a small margin but by a huge unbelievable amount.

That being said you as the consumer must know that you should negotiate your mortgage. That should be a given. You need to make a conscious decision to negotiate for the best possible mortgage you can get. You have been given the knowledge and the inside information to be able to do so.

I still don't understand how consumers will spend weeks and weeks shopping and negotiating for a $15,000 automobile and go through what I would consider to be excruciating agony, but for a $200,000 dollar mortgage that will cost them well over $400,000 over the life of the mortgage they refuse to put in the same effort they did with their automobile. It just makes no sense to me!

So be prepared to negotiate! I have not seen too many people men or women that go to an auto dealership and just pay sticker price. It is such a common practice in the auto industry to negotiate, that the industry has adapted to it and most do not even put the price of the vehicles on the autos. You didn't think that was an accident did you? It is done for several reasons. One being the fact that they want a trained salesperson to have an opportunity to be able to speak (Sell) with you regarding the vehicle to increase the odds of you buying the auto and at the price they want.
The industry has gotten so adapted to this type of sales tactic that in my opinion, they have single handedly changed the way most consumers look at sales people. They have given themselves such a bad reputation that the fraze "used car salesman" is used in many sales industries by many millions of people as a negative description of who they are not and what they don't want to be treated like.

Think about it. They not only not post the prices of the autos on their lot, but they give so many people different prices for the same auto. Once again they have in my opinion created another very negative connotation for all sales people with the negative but true term, switch and bait! Sad but true.

So why is it, that almost 100% of consumers have been programmed and trained to immediately negotiate for a new or used auto that is no where near the price of their mortgage? With their mortgage, they rarely if ever even attempt to negotiate for their mortgage. And I quite frankly am hoping to have a huge affect with that reality.

*"So why is it, that almost
100% of consumers have been
programmed and trained
to immediately negotiate
for a new or used auto that
is no where near the price
of their mortgage?"*

What to say and how to say it

Okay so we've covered the fact that all consumers looking to buy a mortgage for a new home or refinance their current home need to negotiate their mortgage. It should be common practice. Now what?

Now you need to know what to say and how to say it. This is the most common concern and request from most mortgage owners I know. I've created some scripts and rebuttals that you can use in order to negotiate and get the rate lowered and cover some of your closing costs.

These scripts have been proven over time and have been directly responsible for saving mortgage owners tens of millions of dollars on closing costs and most likely hundreds of millions of dollars on interest payments. These are very powerful scripts that can and will save you money. Use them on your next mortgage!

Before you use these scripts you must know the following.

These scripts are intended for the use consumers that are in the process of buying a new mortgage or refinancing their current mortgage. These scripts are also intended once a consumer has been shopping around for the right mortgage and once they have some quotes in the form of Good Faith Estimates (GFE's) from 2-3 lenders, brokers or mortgage professionals.

This way when you use the scripts the mortgage professional will know that you mean business and they will not want to loose your business and you'll get the mortgage you want at a lower rate than you were originally quoted and at lower closing costs than you also were quoted.

Getting Some Quotes

Don't forget that you should not allow each of these mortgage professionals to pull your credit. This could lower your credit scores between 5-8 points each time your credit is pulled. Once you know exactly what mortgage you want, need and can qualify for, you should let the mortgage professional to put together a mortgage quote along with a 1003 application and Good Faith Estimate (GFE). When you're asking for these items, you'll also be asking for the exact mortgage you already have a good idea you qualify for.

So as an example, you'll be asking for an FHA 1/1 ARM. Or a 3/1 Conventional. You'll be asking for these mortgages knowing exactly what you are saying. This will give you some leverage right from the start.

They'll know you either know what you are talking about, have someone you know (Me) in the business who is coaching you or that you have done a heck of a lot of shopping around and are becoming very knowledgeable. They will know that you have put in your due diligence and will not want to scare you or loose you before they have even had a chance to attempt to sell you.

Make sense?

Please also know that it never costs too much for great service! It also will never cost too much when you are dealing with the right mortgage professional. The one that will allow you to sleep at night knowing he knows what he's doing and that he will get you the best possible mortgage for your situation and he has the resources available to get you what you need and want. It will cost you more, but the benefits will greatly out way not dealing or paying for the right professional.

If a consumer called me asking for this situation, I would never just quote a rate or closing costs before I know exactly what I'm looking at and dealing with. I'm a professional whose time is very valuable and I don't waste my time with just anyone and I definitely don't work with just anyone. I also know my value and what I can do for my clients, and I deserve every penny I earn from the mortgages I sell. So unless you know a true mortgage professional as myself, then these scripts will help you get what I would get my clients from the beginning.

Don't get discouraged if you get a hold of someone like myself, because they will be the ones you'll want to do business with. You'll know who that mortgage professional is when you speak with them. They'll lay it out for you.

That being said doesn't mean that you should purposely try to seek out someone like myself. They are few and in between, but with these scripts you'll be able to search out qualified mortgage professionals that will be able to help you out, but only if you apply the principals you've learned from this book.

Before you ask for a quote to be faxed or mailed to you, remember one thing. Know what you are asking for, that will give you the leverage of getting the best possible rate and closing costs. If you do not know what you should ask for the mortgage professional will know that you really don't know what you are asking for but are trying to sound like you know what you are talking about and they will most likely take advantage of you and give you something that is not the best possible rate and closing costs for you.

Asking for a quote Script

Hi (Mortgage Professionals Name), this is (Your Name) and I'm calling because I'd like to see what kind of rate and closings costs you have for a (Mortgage Type, FHA, VA, Conventional, etc.) with an (Interest Rate Type, Fixed, 1/1, 3/1, 5/1, etc.)

Can you (Fax me, Mail me) a 1003 (Ten-0-3) with a Good Faith Estimate (GFE)?

After Receiving the Quote Script

Hi (Mortgage Professional Name) this is (Your Name).
I received the 1003 (Ten-0-3) that you sent me. Thanks I appreciate that. I would like to go over a few things with you. Do you have a moment?
If Yes…Continue
If no…Okay (Mortgage Professional Name) when would be a better time for us to go over a few things?

Okay Great! So I looked everything over and I actually have a couple of other Good Faith Estimates (GFE) from a couple of other mortgage companies. All I'm looking for is the best possible mortgage with the lowest rate and closing costs for me. I'm just looking out for my best interest. I hope you can appreciate that?

So what are you willing to do on the rate? And also the closing costs or the origination fee?

Note:
You should be expecting a rate reduction of an 1/8 (.125%) to a quarter (.25%). There should also be a drop in the origination fee which is typically 1.00% to .75% or even .50%. If both of these do not happen, let them know that you do not have any incentive to move forward with them.

Negotiating Rate and Closing Costs Script

Okay (Mortgage Professional Name),
I saw your quote. It does not look too bad, but I am concerned about the rate and closing costs. I have a couple of other Good Faith Estimates, and one of them has a lower rate and about the same in closing costs. Another one has a higher rate, but lower closing costs. So what I'm looking for you to match the lower rate and closing costs. If you will lower your rate and closing costs, I'll be ready to move forward!!

Note:
Anything other than them complying with your request should warrant more negotiation and or not moving forward! Regardless of what they say, even if it is the best deal and even if you will move forward with them. DO NOT MOVE FORWARD ON THIS CALL!! If they do not comply, do not move forward on this call. Tell them you will get back with them. This will call their bluff. If they are 100% serious and cannot go any lower, they will stick to their guns and when you call back tomorrow, to ask again what they can do. They

will either lower both, or stick with their guns. Then and only then should you move forward.

Accepting their Offer Script

Can I speak with (Mortgage Professionals Name)?

Ho (Mortgage Professionals Name), this is (Your Name), I was going over your figures again and wanted to see if you have had a chance to see what you can do about the ragte and closing costs?

(Pause? Let them think for a moment and wait until they answer)
If you like what you hear and they have lowered the rate or closing costs or both, then you should make the final decision now and move forward or not. But the negotiating is over. They either will or won't, but move forward one way or the other. With them or with out them. Once you have made the decision to move forward, stick with it and stop shopping around or trying to negotiate. This will only cause you more stress and also cause the mortgage professional to not want to work with you! Neither is good.

Remember, that getting the best possible mortgage for yourself will require you to follow these proven methods. It will take effort on your part. You should also remember not to move forward if you have not been able to get a lower rate or closing costs or both from their initial quote.

A sale is the negotiation of the sale. All sales should be a win-win. A win situation for the consumer (You) and a win situation for the mortgage professional and company. Also remember that almost 100% of salespeople including mortgage professionals do not give you the best deal the first time around. That gives them leverage to negotiate if and when it is needed. So know, that almost 100% of the quotes you will get at first are not the best one for you. It's just like the infamous sticker price on an auto. It is almost always negotiable. Heck, most automobile salespeople will even tell you when they tell you the price. Oh the price of this car is (Amount) but don't worry, we can work on that! That sounds so silly doesn't it. The reason for this is that the automobile salespeopled have heard so often how consumers are now on to them and have heard so much, that they include in their rebuttals, what it is they already know they are going to hear? Make sense?

It is silly, but the automobile industry hasn't changed their sales tactics, which is sad to see. It is like the switch and bait which the auto industry invented. It took a long time for them to discover new ways of selling, and now they must come up with another new way of adapting to the changing consumers and times. Some have, as you have probable seen. The "No Haggle Sticker Price".

But this is a mortgage book, so remember. I'm giving you the inside trade secrets that will get you the best possible mortgage for you and your family. This information is way overdue in my opinion and way ahead of its time at the same time. So use it wisely!

"These scripts have been proven over time and have been directly responsible for saving mortgage owners tens of millions of dollars on closing costs and most likely hundreds of millions of dollars on interest payments"

Contacting the author

The author Oliver P. Maldonado can be retained to consult with your organization to help train your sales and marketing staff. Oliver P. Maldonado is an expert in sales & marketing and is one of the most sought after Sales, Marketing & Mortgage consultants in the industry.

Oliver P. Maldonado is also available for speaking engagements.

You can contact the author several different ways. The first is you can call the publishing company 1st Books at 1-800-839-8640 and they can get you in touch with the author. They can also help coordinate speaking engagements along with book signings.

You can also get additional information by visiting the authors website at WWW.OliverMaldonado.com

Contracting the author to train your sales staff

Oliver P. Maldonado industry expert, mortgage consultant, top producer and sales trainer can be contracted to consult with your sales and marketing staff to increase your lead generation, referrals or new application production which will increase the overall production in your organization. What ever your needs and desires are Oliver P. Maldonado can help increase the weekly, monthly and yearly production to what ever level you can handle. If the loan officers in your organization need an extra 15 new mortgage applications per month, week or day, Oliver P. Maldonado can help them get it. If you would like to generate over 100 new mortgage applications per week, or even if your needs are higher than that and you would like to generate over 1,000 new mortgage applications per month! Oliver P. Maldonado can be retained to consult for your organization to achieve your goals!

Oliver P. Maldonado has consulted and generated very successful sales and marketing campaigns for other industries as well. Industries such as satellite dish, financial planning, insurance, home and business alarm systems, cellular phone and the health fitness industry to mention just a few.

Oliver P. Maldonados expertise in sales & marketing and the mortgage industry currently generate personal yearly volume of over $3 billion in mortgage applications and over $200 million in closed loans annually.

Contracting the author to set up a marketing campaign

Oliver P. Maldonado has consulted for over 50 national known mortgage organizations and has helped them set up new marketing and sales campaigns.
He has personally trained hundreds if not thousands of sales professionals not only in the mortgage industry but for many sales organizations.

Oliver has set up sales and marketing offices around the country and has personally opened from scratch over 60 new offices in 30 states.

Oliver P. Maldonado is a true sales and marketing expert and has a proven track record using his sales and marketing systems and techniques.

You can also visit the authors website at
WWW.OliverMaldonado.com

How to generate as much mortgage leads and sales as you can handle

Oliver P. Maldonado has developed a proven fail proof sales and marketing campaign for small to medium sized mortgage companies. His system has also been tested and proven successful with insurance companies, satellite cable, cellular services and alarm companies. While Oliver P. Maldonado has developed proven sales and marketing campaigns for many different organizations, he's currently consulting for companies in the mortgage industry but will also be accepting new consulting contracts in other industries as well.

As an example, with a minimum staff of only 3 Lead Generators Oliver P. Maldonado can set up a sales and marketing campaign that will generate 100 new mortgage applications per week. That's about $15 Million ($15,000,000) per week in new mortgage applications!

Yes you read that right. That can be generated with a minimal staff of only 3 lead generators!

If you are serious about growing your company!
You will need to generate new business and sales for your company. If you are serious about generating new business and sales for your organization?
You will need an industry expert that has already generated proven systems and campaigns to do it.

If you are SERIOUS about growing your company and making a lot of money you need someone that can help you get there! You need Oliver P. Maldonado!

Glossary and Mortgage Terms

Mortgage Terms

203(b): An FHA program that provides mortgage insurance (MI) to protect lenders from the default of the borrowers; used to finance the purchase of new or existing one- to four family housing; characterized by low down payment, flexible qualifying guidelines, limited fees, and a limit on maximum loan amount. **203(k):** An FHA mortgage insurance (MI) program that enables homebuyers to finance both the purchase of a house and the cost of its rehabilitation through a single mortgage loan.

A

Acceleration Clause
A clause in your mortgage which allows the lender to demand payment of the outstanding loan balance for various reasons. The most common reasons for accelerating a loan are if the borrower defaults on the loan or transfers title to another individual without informing the lender.

Adjustable-Rate Mortgage (ARM)
A mortgage in which the interest changes periodically, according to corresponding fluctuations in an index. All ARMs are tied to indexes.

Adjustment Date
The date the interest rate changes on an adjustable-rate mortgage.

Amortization
The loan payment consists of a portion which will be applied to pay the accruing interest on a loan, with the remainder being applied to the principal. Over time, the interest portion decreases as the loan balance decreases, and the amount applied to principal increases so that the loan is paid off (amortized) in the specified time.

Amortization Schedule

A table which shows how much of each payment will be applied toward principal and how much toward interest over the life of the loan. It also shows the gradual decrease of the loan balance until it reaches zero.

Annual Percentage Rate (APR)

This is not the note rate on your loan. It is a value created according to a government formula intended to reflect the true annual cost of borrowing, expressed as a percentage. It works sort of like this, but not exactly, so only use this as a guideline: deduct the closing costs from your loan amount, then using your actual loan payment, calculate what the interest rate would be on this amount instead of your actual loan amount. You will come up with a number close to the APR. Because you are using the same payment on a smaller amount, the APR is always higher than the actual not rate on your loan.

Application

The form used to apply for a mortgage loan, containing information about a borrower's income, savings, assets, debts, and more. The mortgage application is also known as the URLA (Universal Residential Loan Application) and 1003.

Appraisal

A written value (justification) of the price paid or the value for a property, primarily based on an analysis of comparable sales of similar homes nearby.

Appraised Value

An opinion by an appraiser of a property's fair market value, based on his or her knowledge, experience, and analysis of the property.

Appraiser

A licensed individual qualified by education, training, and experience to estimate the value of real property and personal property.

Appreciation

The increase in the value of a property due to changes in market conditions, inflation, or other causes.

Assessed Value
The valuation placed on property by a public tax assessor for purposes of taxation. This value will typically be lower than the actual property value.

Assessment
The placing of a value on property for the purpose of taxation.

Assessor
A public official who establishes the value of a property for taxation purposes.

Asset
Items of value owned by an individual. Assets that can be quickly converted into cash are considered "liquid assets." These include bank accounts, stocks, bonds, mutual funds, and so on. Other assets include real estate, personal property, and debts owed to an individual by others.

Assignment
When ownership of your mortgage is transferred from one company or individual to another, it is called an assignment.

Assumable Mortgage
A mortgage that can be assumed by the buyer when a home is sold. Usually, the borrower must "qualify" in order to assume the loan.

Assumption
The term applied when a buyer assumes the seller's mortgage.

B

Balloon Mortgage
A mortgage loan that requires the remaining principal balance be paid at a specific point in time. For example, a loan may be amortized as if it would be paid over a thirty year period, but requires that at the end of the Fifteenth year the entire remaining balance must be paid. Example a 30 year mortgage due in 15 years (30/15).

Balloon Payment
The final lump sum payment that is due at the termination of a balloon mortgage.

Bankruptcy

By filing in federal bankruptcy court, an individual or individuals can restructure or relieve themselves of debts and liabilities. Bankruptcies are of various types, but the most common for an individual seem to be a "Chapter 7 No Asset" bankruptcy which relieves the borrower of most types of debts. A borrower cannot usually qualify for an "A" paper (Conforming) loan for a period of two years after the bankruptcy has been discharged and requires the re-establishment of an ability to repay debt.

Bill of Sale

A written document that transfers title to personal property after a sale. Example, when selling an automobile to acquire funds which will be used as a source of down payment or for closing costs, the lender will usually require the bill of sale (in addition to other items) to help document this source of funds.

Bi-Weekly Mortgage

A mortgage payment schedule in which you make payments every two weeks instead of once a month. The basic result is that instead of making twelve monthly payments during the year, you make thirteen. The extra payment reduces the principal, substantially reducing the time it takes to pay off a thirty year mortgage. The Bi-Weekly Mortgage is not a mortgage at all, but a mortgage payment schedule.

Bond Market

Usually refers to the daily buying and selling of treasury bonds. Lenders follow this market intensely because as the yields of bonds go up and down, mortgage interest rates do approximately the same thing. The same factors that affect the Treasury Bond market also affect mortgage rates at the same time. That is why rates change daily, and in a volatile market can and do change during the day also.

Bridge Loan

Not used much anymore, bridge loans are obtained by those who have not yet sold their previous property, but must close on a purchase property. The bridge loan becomes the source of their funds for the down payment. One reason for their fall from favor is that there are more and more second mortgage lenders now that will lend at a high loan to value. In addition, sellers often prefer to accept offers from buyers who have already sold their property.

Broker

Broker has several meanings in different situations. A broker is typically someone who is the middle man and works with many other lenders and banking institutions and brokers the loan out to other companies. As a normal definition, a broker is anyone who acts as an agent, bringing two parties together for any type of transaction and earns a fee for doing so.

Buy-down

Usually refers to an interest rate that is being or was bought down to a lower rate in the form of a discount point, or a percentage there of.

C

Cap

Adjustable Rate Mortgages have fluctuating interest rates, but those fluctuations are usually limited to a certain amount. Those are called caped amounts which a rate is capped out at and cannot be adjusted higher than the capped amount.

Cash-out Refinance

When a borrower refinances his or her mortgage at a higher amount than the current loan balance with the intention of getting the remaining difference back out for personal use, is referred to as a "cash out refinance."

Certificate of Deposit

A time deposit held in a bank which pays a certain amount of interest to the depositor.

Certificate of Eligibility

A document issued by the Veterans Administration that certifies a veteran's eligibility for a VA loan.

Certificate of Reasonable Value (CRV)

Once the appraisal has been performed on a property being bought with a VA loan, the Veterans Administration issues a CRV.

Clear Title
A title that is free of liens or legal questions as to ownership of the property.

Closing
This has different meanings in different states. In some states a real estate transaction is not consider "closed" until the documents record at the local recorders office. In others, the "closing" is a meeting where all of the documents are signed.

Closing Costs
Closing costs are separated into what are called "non-recurring closing costs" and "pre-paid items." Non-recurring closing costs are any items which are paid just once as a result of buying the property or obtaining a loan. "Pre-paids" are items which recur over time, such as property taxes and homeowners insurance. These costs are broken down on the Good Faith Estimate which they must issue to the borrower.

Closing Statement
See Settlement Statement.

Co-Borrower
A co-borrower is the 2nd person on the application and is obligated on the loan and is on title to the property.

Collateral
In a home loan, the property is the collateral. The borrower risks losing the property if the loan is not repaid according to the terms of the mortgage or deed of trust.

Collection
When a borrower falls behind, the lender contacts them in an effort to bring the loan current. The loan goes to "collection." As part of the collection effort, the lender must mail and record certain documents in case they are eventually required to foreclose on the property.

Commission
Most salespeople earn commissions for the work that they do and there are many sales professionals involved in each transaction, including Realtors, loan officers, title representatives, attorneys, escrow representative, and representatives for pest companies, home warranty companies, home inspection companies,

insurance agents, and more. The commissions are paid out of the charges paid by the seller or buyer in the purchase transaction. Realtors generally earn the largest commissions, followed by lenders, then the others.

Common Area Assessments

In some areas they are called Homeowners Association Fees. They are charges paid to the Homeowners Association by the owners of the individual units in a condominium or planned unit development (PUD) and are generally used to maintain the property and common areas.

Community Property

In some states, especially the southwest, property acquired by a married couple during their marriage is considered to be owned jointly, except under special circumstances. This is an outgrowth of the Spanish and Mexican heritage of the area.

Comparable Sales

Recent sales of similar properties in nearby areas and used to help determine the market value of a property. Also referred to as "comps."

Condominium

A type of ownership in real property where all of the owners own the property, common areas and buildings together, with the exception of the interior of the unit to which they have title. Often mistakenly referred to as a type of construction or development, it actually refers to the type of ownership.

Condominium Conversion

Changing the ownership of an existing building (usually a rental project) to the condominium form of ownership.

Condominium Hotel

Also known as "Condotel" is a condominium project that has rental or registration desks, short-term occupancy, food and telephone services, and daily cleaning services and that is operated as a commercial hotel even though the units are individually owned. These are often found in resort areas.

Construction Loan
A short-term, interim loan for financing the cost of construction. The lender makes payments to the builder at periodic intervals as the work progresses.

Contingency
A condition that must be met before a contract is legally binding. For example, home purchasers often include a contingency that specifies that the contract is not binding until the purchaser obtains a satisfactory home inspection report from a qualified home inspector.

Contract
An oral or written agreement to do or not to do a certain thing in which consideration (Money) is involved.

Conventional Mortgage
Refers to home loans other than government loans (VA and FHA).

Convertible ARM
An adjustable-rate mortgage that allows the borrower to change the ARM to a fixed-rate mortgage within a specific time.

Cooperative (co-op)
A type of multiple ownership in which the residents of a multiunit housing complex own shares in the cooperative corporation that owns the property, giving each resident the right to occupy a specific apartment or unit.

Credit
An agreement in which a borrower receives something of value in exchange for a promise to repay the lender at a later date.

Credit History
A record of an individual's repayment of debt. Credit histories are reviewed my mortgage lenders as one of the underwriting criteria in determining credit risk.

Creditor
A person to whom money is owed.

Credit Report
A report of an individual's credit history prepared by a credit bureau and used by a lender in determining a loan applicant's creditworthiness.

Credit Repository

An organization that gathers, records, updates, and stores financial and public records information about the payment records of individuals who are being considered for credit.

D

Debt

An amount owed to another.

Deed

The legal document conveying title to a property.

Deed-in-lieu

Short for "deed in lieu of foreclosure," this conveys title to the lender when the borrower is in default and wants to avoid foreclosure. The lender may or may not cease foreclosure activities if a borrower asks to provide a deed-in-lieu. Regardless of whether the lender accepts the deed-in-lieu, the avoidance and non-repayment of debt will most likely show on a credit history. What a deed-in-lieu may prevent is having the documents preparatory to a foreclosure being recorded and become a matter of public record.

Deed of Trust

Some states, like California, do not record mortgages. Instead, they record a deed of trust which is essentially the same thing.

Default

Failure to make the mortgage payment within a specified period of time. For first mortgages or first trust deeds, if a payment has still not been made within 30 days of the due date, the loan is considered to be in default.

Delinquency

Failure to make mortgage payments when mortgage payments are due. For most mortgages, payments are due on the first day of the month. Even though they may not charge a "late fee" for a number of days, the payment is still considered to be late and the loan delinquent. When a loan payment is more than 30 days late, most lenders report the late payment to one or more credit bureaus.

Deposit
A sum of money given in advance of a larger amount being expected in the future. Often called in real estate as an "earnest money deposit."

Depreciation
A decline in the value of property; the opposite of appreciation. Depreciation is also an accounting term which shows the declining monetary value of an asset and is used as an expense to reduce taxable income. Since this is not a true expense where money is actually paid, lenders will add back depreciation expense for self-employed borrowers and count it as income.

Discount Points
In the mortgage industry, this term is usually used in only in reference to government loans, meaning FHA and VA loans. Discount points refer to any "points" paid in addition to the one percent loan origination fee. A "point" is one percent of the loan amount. Discount points are typically used to buy an interest rate down.

Down Payment
The part of the purchase price of a property that the buyer pays in cash and does not finance with a mortgage.

Due-on-sale Provision
A provision in a mortgage that allows the lender to demand repayment in full if the borrower sells the property that serves as security for the mortgage.

E

Earnest Money Deposit
A deposit made by the potential home buyer to show that he or she is serious about buying the house.

Easement
A right of way giving persons other than the owner access to or over a property.

Effective Age

An appraiser's estimate of the physical condition of a building. The actual age of a building may be shorter or longer than its effective age.

Eminent Domain

The right of a government to take private property for public use upon payment of its fair market value. Eminent domain is the basis for condemnation proceedings.

Encroachment

An improvement that intrudes illegally on another's property.

Encumbrance

Anything that affects or limits the fee simple title to a property, such as mortgages, leases, easements, or restrictions.

Equal Credit Opportunity Act (ECOA)

A federal law that requires lenders and other creditors to make credit equally available without discrimination based on race, color, religion, national origin, age, sex, marital status, or receipt of income from public assistance programs.

Equity

Equity is the difference between the fair market value of the property and the principal amount still owed on its mortgage and other liens.

Escrow

An item of value, money, or documents deposited with a third party to be delivered upon the fulfillment of a condition. For example, the earnest money deposit is put into escrow until delivered to the seller when the transaction is closed. Escrows are also the taxes and insurance that is in escrow.

Escrow Account

Once you close your purchase transaction, you may have an escrow account or impound account with your lender. This means the amount you pay each month includes an amount above what would be required if you were only paying your principal and interest. The extra money is held in your impound account (escrow account) for the payment of items like property taxes and homeowner's insurance when they come due. The lender pays them with your money instead of you paying them yourself.

Escrow Disbursements

The use of escrow funds to pay real estate taxes, hazard insurance, mortgage insurance, and other property expenses as they become due.

Estate

The ownership interest of an individual in real property. The sum total of all the real property and personal property owned by an individual at time of death.

Eviction

The lawful expulsion of an occupant from real property.

Examination of Title

The report on the title of a property from the public records or an abstract of the title.

Exclusive Listing

A written contract that gives a licensed real estate agent the exclusive right to sell a property for a specified time.

Executor

A person named in a will to administer an estate. The court will appoint an administrator if no executor is named. "Executrix" is the feminine form.

F

Fair Credit Reporting Act (FCRA)

A consumer protection law that regulates the disclosure of consumer credit reports by consumer/credit reporting agencies and establishes procedures for correcting mistakes on one's credit record.

Fair Market Value

The highest price that a buyer, willing but not compelled to buy, would pay, and the lowest a seller, willing but not compelled to sell, would accept.

Fannie Mae (FNMA)

The Federal National Mortgage Association, which is a congressionally chartered, shareholder-owned company that is the nation's largest supplier of home mortgage funds. For a discussion of the roles of Fannie Mae, Freddie Mac (FHLMC), and Ginnie Mae (GNMA), see the Library.

Fannie Mae's Community Home Buyer's Program

An income-based community lending model, under which mortgage insurers and Fannie Mae offer flexible underwriting guidelines to increase a low- or moderate-income family's buying power and to decrease the total amount of cash needed to purchase a home. Borrowers who participate in this model are required to attend pre-purchase home-buyer education sessions.

Federal Housing Administration (FHA)

An agency of the U.S. Department of Housing and Urban Development (HUD). Its main activity is the insuring of residential mortgage loans made by private lenders. The FHA sets standards for construction and underwriting but does not lend money or plan or construct housing.

Fee Simple

The greatest possible interest a person can have in real estate.

Fee Simple Estate

An unconditional, unlimited estate of inheritance that represents the greatest estate and most extensive interest in land that can be enjoyed. It is of perpetual duration. When the real estate is in a condominium project, the unit owner is the exclusive owner only of the air space within his or her portion of the building (the unit) and is an owner in common with respect to the land and other common portions of the property.

FHA mortgage

A mortgage that is insured by the Federal Housing Administration (FHA). Along with VA loans, an FHA loan will often be referred to as a government loan.

First Mortgage

The mortgage that is in first place among any loans recorded against a property. The lien in first position.

Rixed-Rate Mortgage

A mortgage in which the interest rate does not change during the entire term of the loan.

Fixture
Personal property that becomes real property when attached in a permanent manner to real estate.

Flood Insurance
Insurance that compensates for physical property damage resulting from flooding. It is required for properties located in federally designated flood areas.

Foreclosure
The legal process by which a borrower in default under a mortgage is deprived of his or her interest in the mortgaged property. This usually involves a forced sale of the property at public auction with the proceeds of the sale being applied to the mortgage debt.

401(k)/403(b)
An employer-sponsored investment plan that allows individuals to set aside tax-deferred income for retirement or emergency purposes. 401(k) plans are provided by employers that are private corporations. 403(b) plans are provided by employers that are not for profit organizations.

401(k)/403(b) loan
Some administrators of 401(k)/403(b) plans allow for loans against the monies you have accumulated in these plans. Loans against 401K plans are an acceptable source of down payment for most types of loans.

G

Government Loan (mortgage)
A mortgage that is insured by the Federal Housing Administration (FHA) or guaranteed by the Department of Veterans Affairs (VA) or the Rural Housing Service (RHS). Mortgages that are not government loans are classified as conventional loans.

Government National Mortgage Association (Ginnie Mae)
A government-owned corporation within the U.S. Department of Housing and Urban Development (HUD). Created by Congress on September 1, 1968, GNMA performs the same role as Fannie Mae and Freddie Mac in providing funds to lenders for

making home loans. The difference is that Ginnie Mae provides funds for government loans (FHA and VA)

Grantor
The person conveying an interest in real property.

H

Hazard Insurance
Insurance coverage that in the event of physical damage to a property from fire, wind, vandalism, or other hazards.

Home Equity Line of Credit (HELOC)
A mortgage loan, usually in second position, that allows the borrower to obtain cash drawn against the equity of his home, up to a predetermined amount. A HELOC is very similar to a credit card account, the difference is the home is collateral and the credit line is the equity.

Home Inspection
A thorough inspection by a professional that evaluates the structural and mechanical condition of a property. A satisfactory home inspection is often included as a contingency by the purchaser.

Homeowners' Association
A nonprofit association that manages the common areas of a planned unit development (PUD) or condominium project. In a condominium project, it has no ownership interest in the common elements. In a PUD project, it holds title to the common elements.

Homeowner's Insurance
An insurance policy that combines personal liability insurance and hazard insurance coverage for a dwelling and its contents.

Homeowner's Warranty
A type of insurance often purchased by homebuyers that will cover repairs to certain items, such as heating or air conditioning, should they break down within the coverage period. The buyer often requests the seller to pay for this coverage as a condition of the sale, but either party can pay.

HUD median income

Median family income for a particular county or metropolitan statistical area (MSA), as estimated by the Department of Housing and Urban Development (HUD).

HUD-1 settlement statement

A document that provides an itemized listing of the funds that were paid at closing. Items that appear on the statement include real estate commissions, loan fees, points, and initial escrow (impound) amounts. Each type of expense goes on a specific numbered line on the sheet. The totals at the bottom of the HUD-1 statement define the seller's net proceeds and the buyer's net payment at closing. It is called a HUD1 because the form is printed by the Department of Housing and Urban Development (HUD). The HUD1 statement is also known as the "closing statement" or "settlement sheet."

J

Joint Tenancy

A form of ownership or taking title to property which means each party owns the whole property and that ownership is not separate. In the event of the death of one party, the survivor owns the property in its entirety.

Judgment

A decision made by a court of law. In judgments that require the repayment of a debt, the court may place a lien against the debtor's real property as collateral for the judgment's creditor.

Judicial Foreclosure

A type of foreclosure proceeding used in some states that is handled as a civil lawsuit and conducted entirely under the auspices of a court. Other states use non-judicial foreclosure.

jumbo loan

A loan that exceeds Fannie Mae's and Freddie Mac's loan limits, currently at $322,700. Also called a nonconforming loan. Freddie Mac and Fannie Mae loans are referred to as conforming loans.

L

Late Charge
The penalty a borrower must pay when a payment is made a stated number of days. On a first trust deed or mortgage, this is usually fifteen days.

Lease
A written agreement between the property owner and a tenant that stipulates the payment and conditions under which the tenant may possess the real estate for a specified period of time.

Leasehold Estate
A way of holding title to a property wherein the mortgagor does not actually own the property but rather has a recorded long-term lease on it.

Lease Option
An alternative financing option that allows home buyers to lease a home with an option to buy. Each month's rent payment may consist of not only the rent, but an additional amount which can be applied toward the down payment on an already specified price.

Legal Description
A property description, recognized by law, that is sufficient to locate and identify the property without oral testimony.

Lender
A term which can refer to the institution making the loan or to the individual representing the firm. For example, loan officers are often referred to as "lenders."

Liabilities
A person's financial obligations. Liabilities include long-term and short-term debt, as well as any other amounts that are owed to others.

Liability Insurance
Insurance coverage that offers protection against claims alleging that a property owner's negligence or inappropriate action resulted in bodily injury or property damage to another party. It is usually part of a homeowner's insurance policy.

Lien
A legal claim against a property that must be paid off when the property is sold. A mortgage or first trust deed is considered a lien.

Life Cap
For an adjustable-rate mortgage (ARM), a limit on the amount that the enterest rate can increase or decrease over the life of the mortgage.

Line of Credit
An agreement by a commercial bank or other financial institution to extend credit up to a certain amount for a certain time to a specified borrower.

Liquid Asset
A cash asset or an asset that is easily converted into cash.

Loan
A sum of borrowed money (principal) that is generally repaid with interest.

Loan Officer
Also referred to by a variety of other terms, such as lender, loan representative, loan "rep," account executive, and others. The loan officer serves several functions and has various responsibilities: they solicit loans, they are the representative of the lending institution, and they represent the borrower to the lending institution.

Loan Origination
How a lender refers to the process of obtaining new loans.

Loan Servicing
After you obtain a loan, the company you make the payments to is "servicing" your loan. They process payments, send statements, manage the escrow/impound account, provide collection efforts on delinquent loans, ensure that insurance and property taxes are made on the property, handle pay-offs and assumptions, and provide a variety of other services.

Loan-to-Value (LTV)
The percentage relationship between the amount of the loan and the appraised value or sales price (whichever is lower).

Lock-in

An agreement in which the lender guarantees a specified interest rate for a certain amount of time at a certain cost.

Lock-in period

The time period during which the lender has guaranteed an interest rate to a borrower.

M

Margin

The difference between the interest rate and the index on an adjustable rate mortgage. The margin remains stable over the life of the loan. It is the index which moves up and down.

Maturity

The date on which the principal balance of a loan, bond, or other financial instrument becomes due and payable.

Merged Credit Report

A credit report which reports the raw data pulled from two or more of the major credit repositories. Contrast with a Residential Mortgage Credit Report (RMCR) or a standard factual credit report.

Modification

Occasionally, a lender will agree to modify the terms of your mortgage without requiring you t refinance. If any changes are made, it is called a modification.

Mortgage

A mortgage is a home loan. A legal document that pledges a property to the lender as security for payment of a debt. Instead of mortgages, some states use First Trust Deeds.

Mortgage Banker

A mortgage banker is a lender who uses their own money to loan on home loans. Also see the section on Lenders for a more complete explanation. A mortgage banker is generally assumed to originate and fund their own loans, which are then sold on the secondary market, usually to Fannie Mae, Freddie Mac, or Ginnie Mae. Some firms use this term rather loosely to refer to themselves, whether they are true mortgage banker or simply mortgage brokers or correspondents.

Mortgage Broker

A mortgage company or individual that originates loans, then places those loans with a variety of other lending institutions with whom they usually have pre-established relationships.

Mortgagee

The lender in a mortgage agreement.

Mortgage Insurance (MI)

Insurance that covers the lender against some of the losses incurred as a result of a default on a home loan. Often mistakenly referred to as PMI, which is actually the name of one of the larger mortgage insurers. Mortgage insurance is usually required in one form or another on all loans that have a loan-to-value higher than eighty percent. Mortgages above 80% LTV that call themselves "No MI" are usually a made at a higher interest rate. Instead of the borrower paying the mortgage insurance premiums directly, they pay a higher interest rate to the lender, which then pays the mortgage insurance themselves. Also, FHA loans and certain first-time homebuyer programs require mortgage insurance regardless of the loan-to-value.

Mortgage Insurance Premium (MIP)

The amount paid by a mortgagor for mortgage insurance, either to a government agency such as the Federal Housing Administration (FHA) or to a private mortgage insurance (MI) company. All FHA's have MIP regardless of Loan To Value.

Mortgage Life and Disability Insurance

A type of term life insurance often bought by borrowers. The amount of coverage decreases as the principal balance declines. Some policies also cover the borrower in the event of disability. In the event that the borrower dies while the policy is in force, the debt is automatically satisfied by insurance proceeds. In the case of disability insurance, the insurance will make the mortgage payment for a specified amount of time during the disability. Be careful to read the terms of coverage, however, because often the coverage does not start immediately upon the disability, but after a specified period, sometime forty-five days.

Mortgagor
The borrower in a mortgage agreement.

Multidwelling Units
Properties that provide separate housing units for more than one family, although they secure only a single mortgage.

N

No cash-out refinance
A refinance transaction which is not intended to put cash in the hand of the borrower. Instead, the new balance is calculated to cover the balance due on the current loan and any costs associated with obtaining the new mortgage. Often referred to as a "rate and term refinance."

No-Cost Loan
Many lenders offer loans that you can obtain at "no cost." You should inquire whether this means there are no "lender" costs associated with the loan, or if it also covers the other costs you would normally have in a purchase or refinance transactions, such as title insurance, escrow fees, settlement fees, appraisal, recording fees, notary fees, and others. These are fees and costs which may be associated with buying a home or obtaining a loan, but not charged directly by the lender. Keep in mind that, like a "no-point" loan, the interest rate will be higher than if you obtain a loan that has costs associated with it.

Note
A legal document that obligates a borrower to repay a mortgage loan at a stated interest rate during a specified period of time.

Note Rate
The interest rate stated on a mortgage note.

No-Cost Loan
Many lenders offer loans at "no points." You will find the interest rate on a "no points" loan is higher than on a loan where you pay one point. You will pay more in the long run than the short run with a no cost loan.

Notice of Default
A formal written notice to a borrower that a default has occurred and that legal action may be taken.

O

Original Principal Balance
The total amount of principal owed on a mortgage before any payments are made.

Origination Fee
The origination fee is a standard fee equal to a percentage point typically one percent of the loan amount, but additional points may be charged which are called "discount points." One point equals one percent of the loan amount. On a conventional loan, the loan origination fee refers to the total number of points a borrower pays.

Owner Financing
A property purchase transaction in which the property seller provides all or part of the financing.

P

Personal Property
Any property that is not real property.

PITI
This stands for principal, interest, taxes and insurance. Although all mortgages have PITI the question is whether the taxes & insurance are included in your mortgage payment or not.

PITI reserves
A cash amount that a borrower must have on hand after making a down payment and paying all closing costs for the purchase of a home. The principal, interest, taxes, and insurance (PITI) reserves must equal the amount that the borrower would have to pay for PITI for a predefined number of months.

Planned Unit Development (PUD)
A type of ownership where individuals actually own the building or unit they live in, but common areas are owned jointly with the

other members of the development or association. Contrast with condominium, where an individual actually owns the airspace of his unit, but the buildings and common areas are owned jointly with the others in the development or association.

Point

A point is 1 percent of the amount of the mortgage.

Power of Attorney

A legal document that authorizes another person to act on one's behalf. A power of attorney can grant complete authority or can be limited to certain acts and/or certain periods of time.

Pre-Approval

A loosely used term which is generally taken to mean that a borrower has completed a loan application and provided debt, income, and savings documentation which an underwriter has reviewed and approved. A pre-approval is usually done at a certain loan amount and making assumptions about what the interest rate will actually be at the time the loan is actually made, as well as estimates for the amount that will be paid for property taxes, insurance and others. A pre-approval applies only to the borrower. Once a property is chosen, it must also meet the underwriting guidelines of the lender. Contrast with pre-qualification

Prepayment

Any amount paid to reduce the principal balance of a loan before the due date. Payment in full on a mortgage that may result from a sale of the property, the owner's decision to pay off the loan in full, or a foreclosure. In each case, prepayment means payment occurs before the loan has been fully amortized.

Prepayment Penalty

A fee that may be charged to a borrower who pays off a loan before it is due.

Pre-qualification

This usually refers to the loan officer's written opinion of the ability of a borrower to qualify for a home loan, after the loan officer has made inquiries about debt, income, and savings. The information provided to the loan officer may have been presented verbally or in the form of documentation, and the loan officer may or may not have reviewed a credit report on the borrower.

Prime Rate

The interest rate that banks charge to their preferred customers. Changes in the prime rate are widely publicized in the news media and are used as the indexes in some adjustable rate mortgages, especially home equity lines of credit. Changes in the prime rate do not directly affect other types of mortgages, but the same factors that influence the prime rate also affect the interest rates of mortgage loans.

Principal

The amount borrowed or remaining unpaid. The part of the monthly payment that reduces the remaining balance of a mortgage.

Principal Balance

The outstanding balance of principal on a mortgage. The principal balance does not include interest or any other charges. See remaining balance.

Principal, Interest, Taxes, and Insurance (PITI)

The four components of a monthly mortgage payment on impounded loans. Principal refers to the part of the monthly payment that reduces the remaining balance of the mortgage. Interest is the fee charged for borrowing money. Taxes and insurance refer to the amounts that are paid into an escrow account each month for property taxes and mortgage and hazard insurance.

Private Mortgage Insurance (PMI)

Mortgage insurance that is provided by a private mortgage insurance company to protect lenders against loss if a borrower defaults. Most lenders generally require MI for a loan with a loan-to-value (LTV) percentage in excess of 80 percent.

Promissory Note

A written promise to repay a specified amount over a specified period of time.

Public Auction

A meeting in an announced public location to sell property to repay a mortgage that is in default.

Planned Unit Development (PUD)
A project or subdivision that includes common property that is owned and maintained by a homeowners' association for the benefit and use of the individual PUD unit owners.

Purchase Agreement
A written contract signed by the buyer and seller stating the terms and conditions under which a property will be sold.

Q

Qualifying Ratios
Ratios calculations that are used in determining whether a borrower can qualify for a mortgage. This is also known as the DTI or debt to income ratio.

Quitclaim Deed
A deed that transfers without warranty whatever interest or title a grantor may have at the time the conveyance is made.

R

Rate Lock
A commitment issued by a lender to a borrower or other mortgage originator guaranteeing a specified interest rate for a specified period of time at a specific cost.

Real Estate Agent
A person licensed to negotiate and transact the sale of real estate.

Real Estate Settlement Procedures Act (RESPA)
A consumer protection law that requires lenders to give borrowers advance notice of closing costs.

Realtor®
A real estate agent, broker or an associate who holds active membership in a local real estate board that is affiliated with the National Association of Realtors.

Recording
The recording or noting in the county clerks office the details of a properly executed legal document, such as a deed, a

mortgage note, a satisfaction of mortgage, or an extension of mortgage, thereby making it a part of the public record.

Refinance
Is the process of paying off one loan with the proceeds from a new loan on the same property.

Revolving Debt
A liability or credit account such as credit cards that allow a customer to borrow against a pre-approved line of credit when purchasing goods and services. The liability is revolving since it can be used as much or as little as the consumer would like, so long as the funds are available.

S

Second Mortgage
A mortgage that has a lien in the second position to the first mortgage.

Secondary Market
The buying and selling of existing mortgages, usually as part of a pool or block of mortgages.

Seller Carry-Back
An agreement in which the owner of a property provides financing, often in combination with an assumable mortgage.

Servicer
A company that collects mortgage payments from borrowers and manages borrowers' escrow accounts. The servicer is not typically the actual lender that has given a mortgage.

Servicing
The act of collecting (servicing) mortgage payments from borrowers and related responsibilities of a loan servicer.

Settlement Statement
A statement that has all of the settlement fees also see HUD1 Settlement Statement.

Subdivision
Is housing developments that is created by dividing a tract of land into individual lots for sale or lease.

Subordinate Financing
Is any mortgage or other lien that is being allowed to remain on title in the position after another mortgage typically being the first mortgage and second mortgages are typically the ones being in the subordinate position.

Sweat Equity
Is a contribution to the construction or rehabilitation of a property in the form of labor or services rather than cash.

T

Title
Is a legal document evidencing a person's right to or ownership of a property.

Title Company
A company that specializes in examining and insuring titles to real estate.

Title Insurance
This is insurance that protects the lender (lender's policy) or the buyer (owner's policy) against loss arising from disputes over ownership of a property or mistakes on title.

Title Search
Is a search of the title records to ensure that the seller is the legal owner of the property. A title search will also show any other liens or other claims outstanding.

Truth-in-Lending (TIL)
Is a federal law that requires lenders to fully disclose, in writing, the terms and conditions of a mortgage, including the annual percentage rate (APR). The Truth In Lending is also a mortgage document entitled Truth In Lending.

V

VA mortgage
Is a mortgage that is guaranteed by the Department of Veterans Affairs (VA).

Veterans Administration (VA)

This is an agency of the federal government that guarantees residential mortgages made to eligible veterans of the military services. The guarantee protects the lender against loss therefore encouraging mortgage lenders to make mortgages to veterans.

WWW.OliverMaldonado.com

About the Author

Oliver Maldonado is an industry expert, mortgage consultant, top producer and mortgage sales trainer. His expertise generates a yearly volume of over $3 billion in new mortgage applications and over $250 million in closed loans annually. He's worked with thousands of consumers and has consulted for many of the top mortgage companies in the country.

Oliver Maldonado has also trained thousands of mortgage loan officers and mortgage directors throughout the country on mortgage products.

He's also developed many mortgage programs such as the lowest closing cost and interest rate guarantee where the consumer is guaranteed in writing to have the lowest closings cost and interest rate possible.

He's regarded by many as a leading expert in the mortgage industry.

www.ingramcontent.com/pod-product-compliance
Lightning Source LLC
Chambersburg PA
CBHW031835170526
45157CB00001B/309

* 9 7 8 1 4 1 4 0 3 6 6 5 6 *